THE FAMINE IN IRELAND

Mary E. Daly

Published for the
Historical Association of Ireland
by Dundalgan Press, 1986

First Published 1986
Second Impression 1994
ISBN 0-85221-108-2

FOR PAUL

© Mary E. Daly and the Historical Association of Ireland
Printed by Dundalgan Press, Dundalk

FOREWORD

This is the second in a series of Student Paperbacks published by the Historical Association of Ireland and designed to present to teachers and students of history, as well as to general readers, the findings of specialists in historical research. Dealing with major topics in Irish history, these concise and up-to-date accounts, written by experienced university teachers, should be particularly helpful to students preparing for Leaving Certificate and G.C.E. Advanced Level examinations and to those embarking on the study of history in third-level institutions.

ART COSGROVE
General Editor

Although the famine of the 1840s is one of the central events in modern Irish history, relatively little has been written directly on this subject in recent years. This book is not a comprehensive history of the famine — such a work would require considerably greater time and space — rather it attempts to re-examine the event in the light of current thinking on nineteenth century Irish economy and society. In writing this book I have been heavily dependent on the work of many other scholars and I gratefully acknowledge my debt. Particular thanks are due to David Dickson, Cormac O Grada and Tim O'Neill. Ken Hannigan suggested the source for the cover, which was designed by Jim O'Keeffe of the UCD Audio-Visual Centre, Arnold Horner advised on maps which were produced by Eddie Buckmaster and Liz Whelan of the UCD Geography Dept. Art Cosgrove suggested that I write this book and awaited its completion with his usual patience. Final mention must be of my family, and especially Paul who pressed eagerly for its completion because of a promised dedication. I hope that he will eventually read this book.

MARY E. DALY

CONTENTS

PART I. IRELAND BEFORE THE FAMINE

	Page
Pre-Famine Population	1
Mortality and Food	6
Eighteenth Century Irish Agriculture	10
The Rise of Domestic Industry	11
Land Ownership and Control in Pre-Famine Ireland	13
Social Structure and Living Standards	19
The Standard of Living in Pre-Famine Ireland	31
Pre-Famine Demographic Adjustment	34
A Demographic Crisis in Pre-Famine Ireland?	38
British Government Policy towards Ireland 1815-45	43

PART II. THE FAMINE

Causes of Famine	52
Farmer-Labourer Relations	63
The Changing Structure of Agriculture during the Famine Years	65
The Government's Response	66
Government Famine Relief Policy: Food Depots	69
Public Works	73
Soup Kitchens	87
Society of Friends	89
Poor Law and Famine Relief	92
Famine Deaths	98
Emigration	105
Evictions	109
Conclusion	113

EPILOGUE. THE LEGACY OF THE FAMINE — 117

References	125
Note on Further Reading	138

PART 1

IRELAND BEFORE THE FAMINE

Pre-Famine Population

The Irish famine cannot be viewed as an isolated event. Most commentators have tended to view it as inextricably bound up with Ireland's earlier population growth and the social and economic factors which promoted it. Any understanding of the factors involved in the population loss which took place during the great famine must begin with an exploration of the factors which brought about the rapid population growth of the preceding decades. The picture is somewhat more confused than it appeared in 1950 when Prof. K. H. Connell presented his pioneering analysis and suggested that population growth was the result of a falling age of marriage which in turn led to a higher birth-rate.[1] The superior nutritional qualities of the potato and the availability of waste-land were deemed to have triggered this population explosion.

More recent analysis is both more complicated and more tentative but it has the considerable merit of beginning a break-down of Irish demographic change on a regional basis. Pre-famine Ireland, in contrast to the Connell monolith, now emerges as a country with considerable regional and social contrasts.

Any study of pre-famine population is handicapped by the fact that the first census which is regarded as reasonably accurate was completed only in 1841, the first official census twenty years earlier in 1821. Other countries have compensated for this lack by analysing parish registers to decipher trends in marriages and deaths. On this basis it has proved possible to construct a highly sophisticated profile of population change in early modern France and England. These sources are scarce in Ireland, their use is in its infancy, but it seems improbable that they will yield results as apparently conclusive as those obtained from the English and French registers. The dynamics of Irish population in the early modern period will therefore remain somewhat uncertain.

We do know however that the population of Ireland rose rapidly though with some set-backs from the early seventeenth century. In 1600 Ireland contained a population somewhere between 1.1 and

1.4m.[2] By the end of the century this had increased to approximately 2m. From 1687, population estimates can be derived from hearth-tax returns which permit a greater measure of precision.

PRE-FAMINE POPULATION ESTIMATES[3]

	CONNELL	DAULTREY	Census
1687	2.2	2.0	
1712	2.8	2.0-2.3	
1725	3.0	2.2-2.6	
1732	3.0	2.2-2.5	
1744		1.9-2.2	
1753	3.2	2.2-2.6	
1791	4.8	4.4	
1821			6.8
1831			7.8
1841			8.1

By the mid 1740s the population of Ireland was not much greater than in the 1680s. From that point growth was rapid until the 1820s. After that date there is some suggestion that it tended to tail off though the Irish population continued to rise until the famine.[4]

It is rather difficult, given the lack of precise figures, to establish the factors responsible for this increase. Ireland's doubling of population in the seventeenth century, if correct, is considerably in excess of what was experienced in England or in most of continental Europe.[5] Ireland in 1600 had a population which was primarily located in the east and south-east of the country on the fertile lowlands.[6] The seventeenth century saw several waves of immigration from both Scotland and England: an estimated 170,000 immigrants in the years 1652-72 alone. They came from a country which was facing greater pressure on land and other resources to settle in Ulster and in other parts of Ireland. There was a further heavy wave of immigration in the 1690s in reaction to difficult economic conditions in Scotland.[7] In addition to this immigration there is some evidence of internal migration. Earlier Scottish and English families who had settled in Antrim and east Ulster moved farther west. By the end of the seventeenth century immigration had virtually ceased and from the early eighteenth century a small number of Scottish settlers began to drift from Ulster to North America.[8] While the role of immigration was temporary, it made a major contribution to Ireland's population increase in the seventeenth century.

The seventeenth century population increase was not without its setbacks. The wars and massacres of the 1640s claimed many casualties, though not as many as folk memory might credit. Plague in 1652, brought perhaps by Cromwellian troops, was undoubtedly a major killer; the wars of the 1680s would also have increased the death-rate. Ireland, however, seems to have been relatively free of serious food scarcities.[9]

The early eighteenth century was undoubtedly a more difficult period. The ending of immigration and the beginning of emigration suggest that Ireland had become less attractive to the Scots. The years 1728-9 were marked by famine and epidemics of typhoid, fever and dysentery; smallpox was very severe during the early 1730s and a succession of disastrous harvests towards the end of that decade culminated in a major famine during the years 1739-41. Similar disasters were experienced throughout western Europe during these years, caused by exceptionally severe winters and very heavy frosts which caused crops to fail. This in turn made it impossible to import food in large quantities into Ireland which increased the scale of the disaster. The death-rate from this famine would appear to have been 0.2-0.25m. people — a loss roughly proportionate with that of the great famine of the 1840s. The worst mortality was concentrated in Munster, where Bishop Berkeley of Cloyne spoke of whole villages depopulated in Co. Limerick. Approximately one-fifth of the Munster population may have perished — the impact was possible even greater in this area than the famine of a century later. The northern counties escaped relatively lightly but were subjected to a less serious famine in the years 1744-5 which killed cattle and harmed oats and potatoes.[10]

The harsh circumstances of the 1740s wiped out the population gains of the preceding decades. From the 1750s, however, Irish population would appear to have increased at a rate which was the fastest in western Europe. This increase must be the major focus of our attention as it ended in the famine of the 1840s.

In his pioneering account of Irish population, K. H. Connell laid key responsibility on the Irish birth rate and argued that the Irish population rose because the age at marriage fell and the birth rate showed a consequential increase. This explanation was somewhat unfashionable when first advanced: most European scholars at that stage focussed their attention on the supposed decline in the death-rate. However the most recent work on English population suggests that Connell's explanation of Irish population growth holds generally true for eighteenth century England.[11] Whether it remains correct for eighteenth century Ireland is somewhat debatable.

Evidence on the age at marriage in Ireland before the 1841 census is very limited but it would appear that marriage took place in Ireland in the seventeenth century at an earlier age than was the norm in western Europe where it was delayed until a man could support a family by obtaining land or establishing a trade. The western European average age of marriage was 24-26 for a woman.[12] Figures for families displaced to the west by Cromwell in the 1650s suggest an average age of marriage for women of 20-22.[13] A similar picture is confirmed by a detailed comparative analysis of English and Irish Quaker families which revealed that Irish Quaker women married significantly earlier than their English counterparts with a decidedly higher proportion marrying in their late teens and early twenties.[14] Quakers cannot be regarded as typical of the Irish population as a whole, but the contrast in marriage patterns with their English co-religionists whom they strongly resembled in social characteristics cannot be dismissed. If, as the tenuous available evidence suggests, Irish women married at an early age in the seventeenth and early eighteenth century, the scope for a sharp fall in the age of marriage from 1750 is very limited, though some decline may have taken place in Ulster.

Connell provided considerable anecdotal evidence regarding the early marriage of Irish women, citing evidence from the 1836 *Poor Inquiry* of frequent marriages by girls of fifteen years of age and younger. Such anecdotes, however, are not confirmed by the 1841 census which indicates a mean age of marriage for women of 26 and 29.9 for men. If these figures are representative of what happened in earlier decades they suggest an Irish age at marriage which is similar to western Europe at the time and in fact higher than Britain.[15] It is possible, if not yet proven, that Irish marriage ages may have risen in the years 1800-41, while Joseph Lee, in an effort to reconcile the *Poor Inquiry* evidence with the 1841 Census suggests that, while labourers married at a relatively early age, farmers married later in life. The aggregation of the 1841 Census may mask important social distinctions.[16]

We are on more secure ground when examining the birth-rate, though once again figures for years prior to 1841 are limited. The 1841 census suggests a birth-rate of 38-40 per thousand of the population which is much higher than the English level. Irish married women in 1841 produced more children than their English, or European counterparts. In 1841, at least, the higher marital fertility cannot be explained by early marriages. Irish women marrying at a given age seem to have produced more children than their counterparts in other countries.[17] It is impossible to account for this contrast with any precision. We may rule out contraception in the Irish case. Perhaps we should give credence to contemporary statements which suggest that the Irish had a great love of children; the fact that they cost little to rear; that they afforded security and comfort to parents in their old age.

Part of the high fertility may reflect an apparently high level of infant mortality. Mokyr suggests that in 1841 between 200 and 225 per 1000 of all children born died in the first year of life, a figure much higher than in Europe at the time, but much in line with those of a century earlier.[18] The high infant mortality, by providing an abrupt end to breast-feeding may have given rise to further pregnancies and increased the birth-rate while the knowledge that many children would die may have encouraged parents to have larger families to ensure that some would survive to adulthood.

On the whole, evidence relating to mortality is conclusive. K. H. Connell writes of the period from 1750 to the 1820s as marking a gap in the famines. Harsh conditions still prevailed at regular intervals. Wilde's history of Irish famines, compiled in the 1851 census, records many seasons of freakish weather and epidemics of influenza, fever and other diseases. Crops failed on many occasions; cattle died in large numbers. There were subsistence crises in 1756-7, 1762-3, 1770-1, 1783-4, 1799-1800 and on many occasions in the early nineteenth century, yet at no stage prior to the famine of the 1840s is there evidence suggesting that the Irish population declined. The so-called famine of 1799-1800 is said to have resulted in only 65,000 extra deaths in Ireland as a whole.[19] The years 1816-18, described by one writer as marking the 'last great subsistence crisis of the western world', which resulted in death rates more than 50% above normal in Switzerland, Tuscany and Austria had a relatively limited impact on Irish mortality.[20] Years of heavy excess mortality appear to have been fewer after 1750; food shortages do not appear to have been translated into heavy excess deaths and the long-run death rate was well below the birth rate.

The patterns of mortality in countries such as France in the seventeenth and early eighteenth century suggest considerable peaks in mortality in certain years. Irish parish registers are few in number, those surviving are not necessarily representative of the population as a whole, but they give us some insights into the early modern mortality patterns. In Blaris near Lisburn and Magherafelt, Co. Derry, burial peaks occurred in 1718, 1722, 1725, 1728 and 1733. In 1723 and 1733 burials among the Church of Ireland congregation at Magherafelt were almost double the average level of the twenty years 1716-35 and in four of those years burials exceeded baptisms. Virtually all of the excess mortality in bad years was accounted for by children. In years of excess mortality children accounted for up to 75% of all burials.[21] The hearth-tax evidence for Irish population in the late seventeenth and early eighteenth centuries suggests a high growth of population which was dramatically cut back by years of high mortality.[22] It would appear that in the second half of the eighteenth century, while the underlying trend or 'normal' mortality may not have altered much, the peaks became less pronounced and less frequent. This is apparently what happened in France where the first fall in mortality in the eighteenth century is regarded as[23]

> due to the absence of those major catastrophes which until the beginning or even the middle of the eighteenth century destroyed in a few years, if not months, the surplus accumulated during a few decades free from such calamities.

Our limited parish register records suggest that much of the declining mortality was concentrated among those most at risk: the children. A fall in child mortality would have greater long-term demographic significance than an extension of the life expectancy of adult men or women. More children surviving to adulthood could in a generation lead to a higher number of births. Most children dying in the early modern times succumbed to epidemic diseases such as smallpox, typhoid or dysentery. Falling peak mortality levels suggest that such diseases were proving less critical. The impact of medical science on this process was probably limited. Doctors were few in number in Ireland, mostly concentrated in towns and cities which were much less healthy places than the countryside. They were particularly scarce in remote rural areas; even had they been available their impact is unlikely to have been significant. Hospitals too were concentrated in the larger towns and cities, though the decades immediately prior to the famine saw the establishment of a nationwide system of fever hospitals. This, however, cannot account for any fall in fever mortality in the previous century. The only possible medical advance which is worth consideration is the use of inoculation or vaccination against smallpox.[23] This practice, however, was best established in urban areas: most of the Irish population growth took place in the countryside.[24]

Mortality and Food

Many of the years of heavy mortality, such as 1739-41, were years of food shortage. However, the relationship between food, or the lack of it and mortality is by no means clearcut. Few died directly of starvation, even in the famine of the 1840s. In the early eighteenth century smallpox mortality appears to have risen in years of food scarcity, yet there is no medical evidence that malnutrition increases susceptibility to this disease. Some writers have argued that the population expansion in eighteenth century Europe is directly attributable to a better food supply which resulted in lower mortality, but this case is not universally accepted.[25] Evidence from early eighteenth century Ireland records that food scarcities led to people abandoning their homes to wander in search of food. Hearth-tax returns from the famine-stricken 1740s reveal a decline in house numbers which appears to be proportionately greater than the actual fall in population, suggesting that houses were abandoned as families wandered in search of food.[26] In the process they carried infections into areas which had not hitherto been exposed. Mortality was apparently much greater following two consecutive years of food shortage than it was in the case of one harsh year. The major eighteenth century crises of 1728-9 and 1739-41 occurred in those circumstances, as indeed did the crisis of the 1840s.

The absence of such a clear-cut association between food shortages and mortality crises in the later years of the eighteenth century suggests that people were less inclined to wander in search of subsistence and that Irish society was better able to cope with food shortages than in the past. This may possibly be due to improved trade in food. Many crop failures were localised. The problems of 1739-40 were much more severe in the south of Ireland than elsewhere; if local scarcities could be compensated by importing food from other regions it would ease the impact. Food imports could also be of assistance. There were years of harvest failure in the later eighteenth century, and years of two consecutive failures. The very poor grain harvest of 1769 was followed by a second harvest failure in 1770 but heavy grain imports prevented a sharp rise in food prices.[27] Improved local availability of food, if in restricted quantity, the existence of alternatives to the crop which had failed, and the wherewithal to purchase food could all reduce hunger and the tendency to wander with consequential public health risks.

The relationship between the potato crop and population increase remains both complicated and obscure, as does the timing of the crop's spread in Ireland. The simple case presented by Connell that the potato permitted a much larger number of people to be fed on a smaller acreage of land and so encouraged subdivision and early marriage is no longer accepted in its simplistic form. On the other hand, it is impossible to write Irish population history without touching on the potato, if only because of its direct implication in the tragedy of the famine.

The potato provided an alternative to oats and other grain crops, one which was unlikely to fail in years when grain was scarce. It therefore reduced the risks of famine. Potatoes came into season in the winter — at a time when milk was scarce — easing pressure on food supplies during a hungry time. They grew on soil which was unsuitable for other tillage crops and can therefore be seen as increasing the volume of cultivated land. They were particularly valuable on the wetter, poor quality lands of the west of Ireland where the previous diet was heavily dependent on milk. By freeing families on wet land from the need for a herd of cattle — a sizeable investment — potatoes may have permitted men and women to marry at an earlier age than would otherwise have been the case. In the longer term it undoubtedly permitted the population to expand to levels otherwise impossible. Potatoes permitted a family to be fed on much smaller quantities of land than either milk or grain. Because of the potato the minimum size of subsistence holding was much smaller and this may have prevented land scarcity from bringing population increase to a halt at a lower level. Finally the potato is one of the most nutritious sources of food. In adequate quantities, accompanied by a small amount of green vegetables and milk or butter, it provides all vital dietary requirements and unlike other single-item diets does not lead to any deficiency-related diseases. By ensuring good health the potato may have increased the Irish birth-rate and reduced mortality levels.[28]

The spread of the potato cannot be documented with any precision. It seems to have become established in Munster on a fairly extensive basis during the first half of the eighteenth century. Initially it was probably only one component in a varied diet, providing much of the basic winter food. L. M. Cullen argues that only in the worsening circumstances of the early nineteenth century does it shift from being an important item in diet to becoming, for the labourers and cottiers, virtually the sole item of food. Middling and prosperous farming families always ate a balanced diet of grain, potatoes, milk butter and some meat — even on the eve of the famine, while in Ulster, oats, eaten in the form of porridge, constituted an important item of diet, even for labourers.

Whether the potato can be held to have caused the Irish population growth, or whether it spread in response to population pressure is a debatable point. Cullen has argued that Irish population increase took place independently of the potato; that the expansion in potato acreage followed the growth of population and was a reaction to the event as people sought a foodstuff which required less land. However, Mokyr, examining the data given in the 1841 Census on a county basis, argues that the potato, other things being equal, did allow earlier marriages, a higher birth rate and a greater density of population. His conclusion that the potato clearly was a factor, if by no means the only one, in determining the demographic history of Ireland before the famine is the best assessment currently available on this topic.[29]

Until recently there has been no attempt to analyse the regional patterns in Irish population growth. The first works to hazard this, articles by Daultrey, Dickson and O Grada, reveal both major differences in the performance of various regions and shifts in their relative position over time.[30] Population growth was most pronounced in Ulster at the beginning of the eighteenth century, reflecting the rapid population increase which took place in the 1690s due to immigration. The decades prior to 1740 are characterised by strong population growth in both Ulster and Munster, though both experienced setbacks during that decade, Munster suffering particularly badly in 1739-41. Connaught displays the lowest growth rate at this time. Following the population losses of the 1740s Ulster displays the most rapid recovery but Connaught for the first time experiences a population growth in excess of the national average. The years from 1791-1821 show Ulster dropping from its position as leader in Irish population growth to last place with Connaught moving to the fore. These trends are continued between 1821 and 1841.

REGIONAL PATTERNS OF POPULATION CHANGE 1706-1821[30]
(% per annum)

YEAR		LEIN.	MUN.	ULST.	CONN.	IRL.
1706-12		1.6(3)	2.2(2)	3.4(1)	0.5(4)	2.1
1712-15		1.0(2)	1.1(1)	0.2(4)	0.6(3)	0.8
1725-32		−0.1(2)	0.6(1)	−0.1(2)	−0.4(4)	−0.2
1732-44		−0.6(2)	−3.1(4)	0.4(1)	−0.7(3)	−1.0
1744-9		1.1(2)	2.1(1)	−0.8(3)	−2.3(4)	0.4
1753-91	Either	1.0(4)	1.5(3)	1.8(1)	1.5(2)	1.4
	or	1.4	1.9	2.2	2.1	1.9
1791-1821		1.3(3)	1.6(2)	1.1(4)	2.0(1)	1.4

These provincial statistics mask varied trends within each province, between counties, perhaps within counties. Population would seem to have increased least on the more fertile, long-settled land, most on bogland, upland, former woodland and other marginal land. While these contrasting and shifting patterns of population growth may reflect the random impact of disease, famine, marriage and birth patterns it seems more plausible to assume that they reflect social and economic factors. Changes in agriculture, industry and employment patterns and their impact on patterns of land-holding, all had a major effect on the social structure of pre-famine Ireland.[31]

Eighteenth-Century Irish Agriculture

Cattle farming has traditionally dominated Irish agriculture. Hides were among the major Irish exports in medieval times. Much of the land of Ireland in the early eighteenth century, particularly in the west and parts of the midlands, was devoted to cattle and sheep raising. Co. Roscommon in particular was noted for its large sheep runs and in the early eighteenth century its population may actually have fallen as people made way for sheep.[32] Pastoral farming required relatively little labour, but a considerable amount of capital to obtain entry.

The eighteenth century saw a rapid growth in Irish provision and dairying exports. Irish butter exports by the late 1750s were almost eight times the level of a century previously, while exports of salt pork also showed a considerable increase.[33] The dairying and provision trades were concentrated in Munster and it does not seem a coincidence that this area experienced rapid population growth in the early eighteenth century. Dairying required a more intensive population than cattle and sheep grazing. The rise in pork exports was closely related both to the dairy industry—pigs could be fed with surplus skim milk—and to the expansion of the potato crop. The main food supply for Irish pigs was potatoes.[34]

In the late eighteenth century, the momentum achieved by the provision trade was overtaken by the growth of the Irish grain trade. As a result of population increase and industrialisation, England which had traditionally been a net exporter of corn—including supplies to Ireland in years of scarcity—became a net importer from the 1770s. A sharp rise in corn prices—prices doubled in the half century after the 1760s—led to a significant increase in Irish grain acreage. Irish grain exports soared from the 1780s, though butter exports remained high.[35] Land which had traditionally been used for pasture was now ploughed for grain. This brought in its train a rising potato acreage as a heavily-manured potato crop became an essential part of the crop rotation. Tillage also required a considerably larger labour force than either cattle or dairy farming. Mechanisation at this stage was negligible and large numbers of workers were needed for ploughing, sowing, weeding, harvesting and threshing, all done by hand. It was estimated that a farmer with thirty acres primarily devoted to tillage required the services of three labourers and the assistance of their families at peak times.[36]

Irish tillage farming, which was given a boost by higher prices in the 1770s, was further stimulated by the French revolutionary and Napoleonic wars which cut off continental food supplies to Britain and necessitated the feeding of a large army and navy. Wartime inflation provided a further boost to agricultural prices. While the initial stimulus from a rising British population could be regarded as providing long-term market prospects for Irish farming, much of the wartime boost to Irish farm prices was a purely temporary phenomenon. With the coming of peace in 1815, the reopening of the British market to continental grain imports, the demobilisation of the British army and navy, and the onset of a period of falling prices, the golden age for Irish agriculture, particularly for tillage farming, had ended.

The impact of commercial farming, particularly of the grain trade, was greatest on the better and drier land of the east and south-east. This area was closest to the British market, while access for grain from the midlands was facilitated by the network of canals and river navigations which came into being during the closing decades of the eighteenth century. More remote areas of the west, north-west and south-west suffered from poorer soil, a wetter climate and from greater difficulties in gaining access to export markets because of high transport costs. Because of poor soil conditions, there was not much surplus grain available and what existed was frequently distilled into a more portable and valuable commodity: poteen.[37] Workers living on poorer land reaped some of the benefits of the more prosperous areas by migrating to work as *spailpíní* or migratory labourers during the harvest season. Labourers from Monaghan saved the harvest in Co. Meath; workers from Kerry and West Cork travelled to Tipperary, Limerick and East Cork. Income from this source helped to support families on poorer land;[38] in addition many of these areas developed considerable expertise in domestic textile production.

The Rise of Domestic Industry

Domestic textiles constituted the second major area of expanding employment in eighteenth century Ireland. The growth of the Irish linen industry was one of the major industrial success stories of the eighteenth century. Exports which had totalled 500,000 yards in 1698 reached over 40m. yards by the 1790s and the value of Irish textile exports at this stage was more than 50% greater than the value of all Irish agricultural exports combined.[39] Linen had originated in Ulster. Throughout the eighteenth century it expanded from its heartland in the north-east. The success of the Ulster linen industry was, in the words of one writer, 'a form of adaptation for a region otherwise marginal to the European economy'.[40] From there it spread first into the periphery of the province, then into adjoining areas such as north Leinster and north Connaught. The industry was also found in west Cork and parts of Kerry. By 1780 weaving was of considerable importance in Cos. Antrim, Down, Derry, Armagh, Tyrone and had also encompassed Monaghan, Cavan, Louth, parts of Leitrim, Longford, Mayo, Sligo and Roscommon. Spinning was found in all areas mentioned, and in Cos. Meath and Westmeath.[41] In other areas, particularly the south and midlands, domestic carding and spinning of wool was carried on, though this was primarily for domestic use, as the coarse frieze cloths which were produced were not particularly fashionable. All these industries were located in the countryside, or more precisely within the home. In areas where linen prospered, towns expanded, but their role was as marketing centres rather than industrial locations.

Linen and wool employed both men and women. Weaving — a heavy task on a hand loom — was a male preserve; the lighter spinning was done by women or girls over ten years of age. The typical weaver required several spinners to keep him supplied with yarn so that the involvement of women in the industry was considerable. Linen provided an important source of cash income, which could be earned by both men and women. The ability to weave freed a young man from reliance on either building up capital to acquire a farm, or from waiting to inherit land from his father, while women spinners who worked in their own home were capable of continuing to contribute to family income after marriage. This phenomenon of considerable domestic industrial production in rural and domestic settings — called proto-industrialisation — was experienced extensively in western Europe in the late eighteenth century. Several writers have argued that it encouraged earlier marriages by freeing young people from the constraints of land availability and guaranteeing, with both husband and wife working, that they could earn an adequate family income.[42] Some relationship between the Ulster linen industry and the province's rapid population expansion in the second half of the eighteenth century would seem plausible. In addition to possible impact on marriages and hence on births, the cash income from weaving and spinning ensured that a family could buy food in times of scarcity. The spread of the linen industry in the 1780s into Mayo has been credited by Almquist with a major role in the high density of population found in that county in 1841.[43] The 1841 census records 31,195 female spinners in Co. Mayo, over 100,000 in Connaught as a whole. However Mokyr, while not totally disowning any role for cottage industry in Irish population growth, suggests 'that the actual relations are far more nuanced and complex' than Almquist supposed.[44] Part of the problem in both pieces of analysis may simply be that 1841 is too late a date: by that stage domestic industry in Ireland was in sharp retreat. Nevertheless we cannot dismiss it as without significance in pre-famine Ireland.

There is direct evidence in many instances that the income from textiles permitted families to pay rent on their holdings and to survive on holdings much too small to provide full-time support for a family.[45]

A detailed analysis of the 1841 census reveals the combined importance of both intensive tillage farming and of domestic textiles. They were among the two most important sources of employment at the time and they were complementary. Domestic industry tended to predominate in areas to the north and west; agricultural labouring towards the east and south-east.[46] Both combined to provide employment — whether adequate or otherwise — for the rising Irish population. Both based their workforce in the countryside and each had an important, though differing, impact on the structure of land holding. This is the topic which now requires analysis.

Land Ownership and Control in Pre-Famine Ireland

Most Irish landowners in the eighteenth century were relatively recent arrivals. Wars and penal laws had removed most of the native Irish and Anglo-Irish landowners, except where they conformed to protestantism, though many families survived, albeit with depleted influence, in their native areas. Following the disturbed conditions of the seventeenth century land ownership and estate management proved a relatively hazardous activity. Tenants with sufficient capital to stock a large farm and to pay rent with regularity were few in number. Default on rents and disappearance of tenants were common occurrences and rent collection could pose major problems. A caste of professional estate-agents had yet to emerge. The advice proferred to the owner of the Wandesforde estate near Castlecomer in 1726 was that he should[47]

> let the whole lands at a fixed rent to some one solvent tenant who could keep them in subjection and oblige them to pay their respective rents to him and he be obliged to pay your Lordship your rent without dealing with such a lawless clan who are like the highlanders of Scotland that rob and take acres of grass from each other at their pleasure without leave or paying for it.

Thus was born the middleman. Many landlords opted for the security of a fixed rent and granted long leases to a small number of large tenants or speculators. The leases took various forms. At the most extreme there were leases at fixed rents renewable for ever — to all intents and purposes the sale with a perpetual fixed annual charge of an estate; in other instances leases of long duration, commonly for three lives, were granted. By the middle of the eighteenth century, control, if not formal ownership of land had percolated into the ranks of the middling gentry and the larger tenants, many of English extraction, others descended from the Irish or Old English gentry families.[49] Some of these initially farmed these large holdings directly as grazing farms with the help of a small number of herdsmen. Some found the portions too large to stock and too difficult to control and tended to rent portions of the land to smaller independent farmers. This tendency to subdivide the very large farms was accentuated by the rise of the dairying industry in early eighteenth century Munster. Dairying required a large management and labour force so that larger tenants tended to rent out holdings of 30-40 acres complete with cows to dairymen who paid their rent with a proportion of their butter yield. By the second half of the century, however, dairymen were becoming sufficiently prosperous to buy their own cattle and this practice began to decline.[49]

Reliance on middlemen was given a boost by the difficulties of the 1740s which left landlords with disappearing tenants and defaulting rents. Leases granted at that stage would generally have been for 61 years or three lives, expiring in the early nineteenth century.[50] The rising price of grain relative to cattle from 1760 shifted the balance of Irish agriculture away from large grazing farms to smaller tillage units of 30-40 acres. Large tenants, who had until then directly farmed their holdings as grazing farms, found it more profitable to subdivide. In Ulster the prosperity of the fine linen weavers caused them to offer sums of £1 per acre for well-located small holdings of up to five acres where they could grow potatoes and keep a cow and some pigs. The temptation for the larger tenants to take advantage of this demand was enormous and the pressure from high-earning fine weavers pushed the price of land beyond the reach of not only large graziers, but also of smaller full-time farmers in the so-called linen triangle stretching from Lisburn to Armagh and Dungannon.[51]

In some areas the 1790s marked the beginning of the end of the middleman system. With the granting of votes to catholics it now paid politically-active landlords to grant leases to catholic tenants in order to qualify them for the forty-shilling freehold franchise. On the Downshire estate in Antrim and Down there is evidence by this stage of leases being granted to individual sub-tenants with this purpose in mind.[52] By the turn of the century landlords were tending to grant shorter leases to individual tenants. However, many three-life leases took a considerable time to expire. One granted on a 750 acre estate by Cork landlord Sir George Colthurst in 1770 for three lives to one middleman who then had two tenants was still in operation in 1845. By that date the land contained three hundred inhabitants.[53]

The middlemen are generally regarded as a major force for evil in pre-famine Ireland. While they cannot be wholly exonerated from the charges against them, the case is probably overstated. They cannot be held exclusively responsible for the extensive subdivision and increase of population which happened under their control; there is no evidence that landlords would have acted any differently had they been in charge. The landlords' main grievance against the middlemen was that they prevented them from personally reaping the benefits of sharply rising land prices at the end of the eighteenth century. The trend at the time favoured subdivision and smaller farms, whether the land was controlled by a landlord or a middleman. Nobody voiced any major criticism of subdivision until the depression years after 1815.

Long leases meant, however, that the landlords forfeited most of the benefits of rising land values. On the Downshire estate by the end of the 1790s rents on newly-leased land were almost 400% of the levels of the 1740s and they climbed to a peak of 759% of the 1740 level in the years 1815-19.[54] Landlords managed to capture little of this bonanza unless a fortuitous death meant the termination of a lease. On most estates, 'the overall average level of rents of determinable holdings was well below, and in some instances catastrophically below, the current market price for leased property'. One section of the Hamilton estate of 4,620 acres let to Con O Donnell on a lease of one life in 1764 for £315 per annum was still under lease in 1810, by which stage O Donnell, the middleman, was collecting £1,361 from his sub-tenants.[55] Such events naturally angered landlords.

Much subdivision was the work, not of commercial exploiters but of small to medium-sized farmers faced with the need to provide for their families, and with a realization of the current value of land. They too benefited from long leases. The practice was most pronounced in areas with domestic industry and in the west where the tradition of rundale holdings—large tracts of land held in a quasi-communal fashion within a family—prevailed. Population increase led to the division of all plots of land into smaller holdings to cater for the extra numbers.[56] Those not accommodated in this fashion generally had access to large quantities of waste land which was available free, or virtually free, to those prepared to clear and plant it.

Subdivision took a variety of forms. In some cases a farmer, by subletting a small tract of his land as conacre, could collect a sum which would cover the rent of his whole farm. One Kilkenny farmer who rented nine acres for a total of 22 guineas, sublet four for £28.[57] The majority of subdivision took place within the family where a father split off part of his holding to provide for a son or daughter getting married. In a survey of the Gosford estate details are given of several such instances. One farmer, Andrew Boyde, holding 32 acres, gave 14 acres to one daughter and the remainder was divided between his son and two further daughters. In the course of making provision for his family an adequate farm of 32 acres was converted into four holdings, of 2 acres, 4 acres, 10 acres and 14 acres, all too small, two of derisory size.[58] It would appear that at this stage provision was made almost equally for a daughter as for a son. Isaac Weld, in his survey of Co. Roscommon, noted one man who had given half of his five acre holding to his daughter on her marriage: 'he supposed he should have to divide or give up the remainder when the next daughter was married'.[59]

In his survey of the Gosford estate, William Greig spelled out the consequences of such practices.[60]

> Every subdivision lowers the occupier in the scale of ability, notwithstanding their increased industry, the lower they become the less is the desire or the opportunity of providing for their children otherwise than by sharing the farm with them.
>
> If the farm happens to be held under an old lease and at a cheap rate they may still contrive to live with tolerable comfort, even after the subdivision, but, when the lease expires and higher rents must be paid, misery and privation begin. From being able to keep a pair of horses the division

reduces this to one for each or for the use of several holdings, and even that from the want of pasture or fodder must be given up, and a cow forms the chief treasure, the butter paying a large portion of rent; the owner being happy in retaining the buttermilk and potatoes with the whole or part of the grain crop. If he again subdivides or loses the cow he must then be satisfied with the potato crop alone, the grain and flax crops being barely sufficient to pay his rent, and as from the want of animal manure they are yearly becoming worse and at length from the exhausted state of the lands prove inadequate to pay rents, particularly in bad seasons, beyond this stage misery and ruin are barely avoidable. A large arrear is accumulated which, after long indulgence, cannot be paid, and the holding given up, not only with much loss to the rental but the lands and buildings in bad order. Where the linen and cotton manufacture is vigorously followed the evil may be a little longer averted while the family can be maintained from the whole or greater part of the lands, the tenant depending on the spinning wheel and the loom to pay his rent.

In many instances subdivision could only be sustained by domestic industry, in other cases the tenants of small holdings of five acres or so survived by working as labourers during busy seasons on the holdings of larger farmers.

Subdivision was not a universal practice. It would appear to have been much less common on the medium and larger farms of the better agricultural land. In a comparative survey of Co. Tipperary in the 1650s and 1850s it emerged that while the population in the upland areas had quadrupled, that on the more fertile land had only doubled. The author concluded that 'population control was therefore more characteristic of the better lands'. In those areas 'the impact of institutional controls enforced by the landlords or their officials combined with the vested interests of the more commercially-minded tenants in the better farming areas, exerted a significant influence on the distribution of population'.[61]

As William Greig emphasised, lack of capital was a major factor motivating the smallholders to subdivide. Larger farmers did not cut off a portion of their farm to provide for a daughter's marriage, they gave her a dowry in cash. Surplus sons were provided for by education, preparation for the priesthood, provision of capital to set up a business, or by acquiring another farm. There would appear to have been an inverse relationship between the size and quality of land and the tendency to subdivide.

On these larger commercial holdings there existed another form of subdivision: the cottier system. The labour requirements of tillage farms were considerable. A steady male labour force was needed for much of the year, winter months were spent threshing and ploughing, at peak times women and children were also brought into use. Many farmers met their labour needs by using cottiers or bound labourers: men contracted to work for them throughout the year who would not be tempted to disappear in search of higher wages during peak autumn or spring seasons. A cottier and farmer generally made a two-part bargain. The cottier agreed to work for the farmer for a fixed daily rate; in addition he rented a portion of land from the farmer for a fixed annual sum. There he built a cabin, lived with his family and cultivated his potatoes and perhaps a little oats in spare moments. The rent of this plot was paid by the days worked for the farmer — in what Mokyr has termed 'the secondary land market'[62] cash rarely changed hands. In these areas there also existed unbound or casual labourers who were not contracted to work for a particular farmer but were hired for short periods particularly at peak labouring times. They too rented a plot of conacre on which they grew their subsistence food, or alternatively they cleared a plot on the edge of the bog or some other marginal land. They had even less security than the bound labourers as they had less guarantee of work outside the peak seasons. In addition, as already mentioned, part of the peak season labouring needs of middling and large farming areas was met by migratory labourers from the west and south.

The distinction in terms of subdivision and land holding patterns between the different parts of Ireland emerges from the pre-famine statistics on land holding. In Leinster a very high proportion, in several counties more than one quarter of all holdings, were of less than one acre in size. These tiny labourers' plots were less common in Connaught. However in Connaught and Ulster farms between one and ten acres were more common than in the east of Ireland. If we ignore holdings of less than one acre the mean size of farms was considerably lower in the west than in the east. Most of the smaller farms were located west of a line from Derry to Cork.[63]

This picture of regional contrasts also emerges from Beames' analysis of the 1831 Census. This suggests that the ratio of labourers to farmers varied from 4.54 to 1 in Dublin, 2.91 in Kildare and 2.56 in Meath, with ratios in excess of 1 in Limerick, Westmeath, Waterford, Cork, Wicklow, Kerry, Kilkenny, Louth, Longford, Tipperary, Queen's Co. and Wexford to rates of 0.4 labourers per farmer and less in Fermanagh, Galway, Tyrone, Sligo, Donegal, Mayo

FARM SIZE IN PRE-FAMINE IRELAND[64] (PER CENTAGE)

	Ulst.	Leins.	Mun.	Conn.	Irl.
less 1 ac.	12.6	22.5	16.2	9.2	14.8
1-5 ac.	18.6	21.5	16.5	23.1	19.7
5-10 ac.	24.0	14.8	13.9	28.3	20.5
10-20 ac.	30.4	15.9	17.4	20.8	20.2
less than 20	85.6	74.7	64.0	81.4	75.2

MEDIAN SIZE OF HOLDINGS OVER TWO ACRES IN 1841

| 13.3 | 9.8 | 17.8 | 17.7 | 12.8 |

and Leitrim. The latter county with less than one labourer for every 3 farmers, or 0.31 labourers per farmer, had the lowest ratio in Ireland.[65] In the west and north-west farm labourers were relatively uncommon, labourers, or live-in farm servants, being mostly on farms where there were no children capable of assisting with farm tasks. In these areas farms were subdivided and a significant number of households earned part of their income, perhaps all of their cash income from domestic textiles. Almquist in his analysis of the 1841 Census noted that farm labouring and domestic textiles were complementary: the former strong in the east and south-east, the latter in the west and north-west.[66]

Social Structure and Living Standards

During the period from the 1750s to 1845 the population of Ireland increased at an annual rate of 1.3% per annum. National income would need to have risen by the same amount if average living standards were not to decline. It is probable that the late eighteenth century and the wartime years of the early nineteenth century were a time of economic growth: the cultivation margin was extended, new productive activities such as textile work were extended to a wider section of the population; a more intensive and more productive type of farming was undertaken. In addition the terms of trade moved in favour of Ireland: the price of Irish exports rose by more than the price of major imports.

Information on living standards at this time is very sparse. It would appear that the living standards of Munster dairy farmers rose throughout the eighteenth century — reflecting the growing prosperity of their business. In the early eighteenth century many farmers were forced to rent cows from the dairymen because they could not themselves afford the capital investment; this practice had become rare by the 1770s.[67] The 1740 famine would appear to have threatened farming families with starvation; farmers did not face such a threat in the famine of the 1840s.[68] Farming living standards almost certainly rose throughout the second half of the eighteenth century and the early years of the nineteenth century, particularly if they were the beneficiaries of long leases.

The case of the labourer is rather more doubtful. The population increase of the eighteenth and early nineteenth century was concentrated among the labouring class. For some of the period the expansion of tillage farming meant that their job opportunities increased in line. However, labourers were major victims of rising land prices and, unlike farmers, did not have the benefit of long leases at fixed prices. While their money wages apparently rose during the closing decades of the eighteenth century and escalated more rapidly during the wartime years, the price of conacre apparently rose at an even more rapid rate. In the 1770s in addition to bargaining for the rent of a plot of potato ground, the labourer was frequently offered the right to graze a cow and free turf and the right to gather manure might also be included. As the years passed the extras vanished, while the price of a potato plot rose. In Munster by the 1780s the ownership of a cow among labourers was becoming 'less common'.[69]

The loss of a cow meant the disappearance of the major capital item owned by a labouring family—something that could be sold in an emergency to realise ready cash. Loss of a cow also meant loss of manure which was vital to producing a large crop of potatoes. There are increasing references in the early nineteenth century to labourers hiring potato ground, already manured, from a farmer: this tendency reflected the fact that many families no longer had a cow to produce manure. Loss of a cow also deprived the family of a possible financial side-line from selling a calf or from making butter, while reducing their diet by removing buttermilk—one of its main ingredients.

Labourers' wages varied considerably, being higher at peak seasons such as harvest and planting time and in areas close to towns, or where workers had the option of weaving work. Bound labourers were paid a fixed sum throughout the year; *spailpíní* hired only at busy times got a higher daily rate but this was offset by the insecurity of their employment. Higher rates were paid for heavy tasks such as work on the bogs. By the early nineteenth century—at the peak of the wartime boom—rates would seem to have ranged from a minimum of approximately 6d per day with food to a maximum of perhaps 1/- for harvest work in areas of labour scarcity. By 1815 the average Cork labourer apparently earned 4d to 6d per day with food or 6d to 8d without, while the rent of a cabin with pig run and turf supply would cost from £1-10-0 to £2, or a maximum of £3, with potato ground costing £2-£3 per acre without manure, £4 to £6 if manured.[70] If we assume £5 as the cost of a cabin, turf, garden and an acre of unmanured potato ground, the labourer would have to work for 200 days at the higher rate or a virtually impossible 300 days at the lower rate to pay the rent. Not surprisingly such households relied on whatever extra earnings could accrue from a wife or children as a supplement.

The living standards of smallholders in the west and north, dependent on domestic industry, are more difficult to gauge. In the west the availability of waste ground probably prevented land values from rising unduly, though this was not the case in central Ulster where the high earnings of weavers pushed up the price of small farms. The peak of textile workers' earnings was probably around the turn of the century. At this time cotton weavers could earn in excess of £2 per week,[71] fine linen weavers were unlikely to have earned less. The earnings of more marginal coarse linen weavers would have been much less, however, while spinners do not seem to have earned much in excess of 3d per day. The spread of spinning and coarse weaving from the 1780s may have delayed the onset of declining living standards for the population of the west and may in fact have improved conditions for certain families. This may explain the sharp increase in the population of the west from the 1790s.

The Post-1815 Period

The coming of peace in 1815 posed difficulties for Irish agriculture. There had been a hiccup in the steady pattern of rising agricultural prices in 1812. The coming of peace meant an end to the British government's inflationary policy; the money supply was brought back into line, the issue of paper money was curbed, the gold standard was re-established and the overall price level fell sharply. Agricultural prices tended to fall by more than the overall price level. The fall continued in to the early 1820s and, although prices stabilised in the 1820s, there was a further price decline in the early 1830s. The late '30s led the beginnings of a market recovery.

DUBLIN MARKET PRICES 1812-40[72]

1812-15 equals 100.

	Wheat	Oats	Barley	Butter	Bacon	Beef	Mutton
1816-20	91	89	90	81	80	81	83
1821-25	66	68	66	77	64	60	72
1826-30	75	80	83	62	74	58	67
1831-35	60	62	63	68	65	51	64
1836-40	79	76	75	86	77	64	73

The coming of peace eased continental access to the British market, especially for grain crops which were more suited to drier continental climates. Irish tillage farming benefited to some extent from the continuing operation of the British corn laws which were designed to penalise imports at times of low prices, but Ireland no longer commanded the major part of growing British grain imports. During the period 1811-15 to 1836-40 wheat exports to Britain from non-Irish sources rose five-fold, Irish exports rose only by 125%.[73]

Irish agriculture responded to the difficult post-war conditions by attempting to boost exports in order to maintain cash earnings. Our knowledge of the trends in agricultural exports is bedevilled by the fact that after 1825 customs figures no longer exist because of the creation of an Anglo-Irish free trade area. The continuation of the corn laws, however, meant that accurate statistics exist on the grain trade. Wheat exports rose sharply, with some fluctuations, peaking in the early 1830s. However, exports on the eve of the famine in 1845 were the third highest ever recorded. Oats, the principal Irish grain export, also rose at a rapid rate, the volume peaking later than wheat towards the end of the 1830s. Barley exports, which were much less significant, peaked at approximately the same time as wheat.[74]

The picture for other agricultural products is much less certain. Most analysis has hitherto rested on the figures collected by the Railway Commissioners in 1835 which have now been shown to contain a variety of errors. Butter exports apparently peaked in the early 1820s and thereafter stagnated. The Irish provision trade underwent a definite decline as the market for pork and beef contracted in the absence of a need to feed the British navy. The coming of a steamship service to the Irish sea during the second decade of the nineteenth century opened up the real possibilities of shipping live animals to Britain in large numbers. By 1835 live cattle exports were probably double the level of the early 1820s and had again doubled by the famine years of the mid 1840s; sheep exports rose more than four-fold from the 1820s to the 1830s and again doubled by the mid forties. Live pig exports rose by an even greater volume, while in contrast to the stagnation of the beef and pork trades, exports of bacon also showed a very substantial increase from the 1820s. The other trend worth some brief notice is the rapid expansion of grain exports from northern and western ports. There was also probably an increasing export of provisions from these areas, though provision exports from the west remained small.[75]

It is difficult to interpret the significance of these trends for Irish farming. The decline in provision exports and the growth of livestock exports prefigures what became the main trend of nineteenth century Irish agriculture. However it would not be correct to claim, as Crotty does, that these years marked a definite shift out of tillage in favour of livestock production. Grain exports grew until the 1830s; thereafter they did not sharply contract, rather they fluctuated, with some of the lower figures, notably for the years 1839-42, reflecting bad harvests rather than changing agricultural practices. Irish agriculture on the eve of the famine remained predominantly a tillage agriculture. Even the pig industry should be seen as an offshoot of Irish tillage. Pigs were fed almost entirely on potatoes; the sharply rising pig and bacon exports suggest that the volume of potatoes grown was increasing in the years before the famine—this was certainly so in Co. Cork.[76] Given the importance of potatoes in the rotation of grain crops it is not impossible that the acreage devoted to these crops also rose.

The pre-famine years were marked by a certain amount of land reclamation though its extent is somewhat in doubt. Prof. Connell presented a case, using figures from the 1841 and 1851 census reports, for a substantial level of reclamation, particularly in the west, during the famine decade; and other partial figures indicated considerable reclamation in areas such as Kerry and Donegal in earlier years. However, subsequent analysis by Bourke reveals that the figures on which these calculations are based cannot be viewed as reliable. However,he suggests that land reclamation was proceeding, though at a rate slower than the rise in population.[77]

While Irish agriculture was undergoing certain structural changes in response to market conditions and changing transport systems, it remained overwhelmingly concentrated on tillage. Examination of the volume of agricultural output suffers from the absence of an agricultural census until the eve of the famine. Nevertheless, estimates by O Grada suggest that tillage products accounted for over 63%, almost two-thirds of the volume of agricultural output at this time.

Potatoes accounted for 24% of total output, cattle and milk combined for less than 23%. Excluding the potato, which was primarily a subsistence crop, the bulk of Irish agriculture on the eve of the famine was devoted to crops with a potential cash sale.[78] Irish agriculture was therefore predominantly commercial, rather than subsistence, as is frequently claimed. A comparative analysis by Solar of Scottish and Irish agriculture in the 1850s suggests that Irish agriculture compared not unfavourably with the much-vaunted Scottish farming, with total factor productivity somewhere between 77 and 91% of the Scottish figures.

> Per acre output was higher in Ireland on all three measures of the land input and was likely to have been even higher before the famine. Crop yields in Ireland generally exceed those in Scotland. In the mid-1850s barley yields were on average higher than turnips. Milk yields were probably higher in Ireland.

In normal pre-famine circumstances Ireland was feeding its own farm population, a relatively large population in Irish towns and cities and exporting one-quarter of its output to Britain. Irish agriculture fed in the region of 9-10m. people in pre-famine times.[79]

All was not gloomy therefore in the immediate pre-famine years. Nevertheless, falling agricultural prices and the attempt to readjust Irish farming patterns to changing circumstances posed strains for Irish rural society. Falling prices presented major difficulties for farmers, especially those whose leases had expired during the latter years of the war. On the Downshire estate leases of 40-50 years standing, which expired during the years 1801-15, were renewed at rents 4-5 times their previous level. Such rents proved onerous during the difficult years of the post-famine period. The problems of falling prices were exacerbated by the freakish weather of the years 1816-18. Poor weather and falling prices forced some landlords to abate rents which had been recently set. On the Edenderry estate of the Downshire family new rents were abated by 25%; on their Blessington estate in both 1818 and 1821 — another bad year — rents were reduced by approximately 25%.[80] Landlords who proved unsympathetic to demands for rent abatements would have done well to make some concessions; regardless of their refusal, rent arrears mounted. On the large Fitwilliam estate, situated in the comparatively prosperous counties of Wicklow, Waterford and Kildare, arrears increased from less than £3,000 in 1814 to over £11,000 in 1818 and £35,000 by 1826.[81]

As a reaction to these uncertain condition leases became less common. Those granted tended to be shorter — for twenty-one years or one life, rather than the previous sixty-one years or three lives. The political rebellion of the 40/- freeholders, who defied their landlords in the battle for catholic emancipation, and their subsequent disenfranchisement reduced the political value of granting leases for lives. Tenancy at will became more common, particularly for smallholders. However, it is impossible to discover with precision what proportion of land was held at will or under lease. Mokyr's analysis of returns to the *Devon Commission* suggests that while leases were relatively uncommon in Connaught, they covered 'a substantial minority' of holdings in Ulster and Munster and were common in Leinster. Analysis of the earliest estates sold under the Encumbered Estates Act of 1849 shows that a majority of the larger farms were held under lease.[82] This may not be truly representative: it could be argued that these estates went bankrupt partly because they contained a lot of land held on long lease; estates held at will may have been less likely to wind up in the courts. Mokyr's evidence, however, is sufficient to suggest that leases were by no means uncommon on the eve of the famine, even if his assertion that two-thirds of land was held on long lease may be an overstatement. A study of Westmeath at the time suggests a dual pattern: larger farms in excess of thirty acres tended to be held on lease, smaller holdings were held at will.[83]

We cannot speak with certainty about the ability of farmers to cope with changing economic circumstances. Conditions varied enormously depending on size of farm, quality of land, nature of agriculture practised and the rent and leasing arrangements. Those who were dependent primarily on tillage farming probably suffered some drop in living standards. At least some of the increased oats and other grain exported to England may have come from family tables. As Prof. Cullen has pointed out, commercialisation does not invariably mean a gain to the producer,[84] and the growing export of grain from the west and the north-west, while partly reflecting improved communications, may mean a more monotonous diet at home and the need to realise cash to pay rents. Hard times made it difficult for farmers to accumulate capital. There were few pigs on the Gosford estate by 1820 because they had been sold off during the preceding difficult years.[85] Rent arrears meant tenants in debt with consequential danger of incurring landlord wrath. The traditional method of recovering rent arrears, distraint, the seizure of animals and crops, tended to become unpopular, partly because it could be evaded by driving cattle to a neighbouring farm, and because it was virtually inoperative, and often unjust in cases of rundale farming. In cases of sub-letting, the crops and animals of under-tenants could be seized to meet the debts of the head tenant. After 1816 it became possible to evict a tenant by use of a civil bill, and eviction would seem to have become the common method of landlord redress. It proved useful in cases where a landlord wished to remove a tenant, or to consolidate a farm, but was very ineffective if the purpose was simply to recover rent arrears.

The gradual demise of middlemen gave landlords increasing control over their estates. Prof. Donnelly has argued that the ending of long leases, coupled with the difficult economic circumstances, prompted landlords to take significantly greater interest in estate management, though Cullen sees this as part of a long-term trend evident from the eighteenth century.[86] While many remained passive and distant rent collectors, others began to survey their estates and plan for long-term development. Some began to devote significant sums of money to estate improvement, in marked contrast to the financial neglect of the past. There is little evidence, for example, of the Downshire family spending much on estate improvement before the 1830s when they became involved in land drainage, which was one of the most fashionable investments.[87] However, their maximum expenditure would not seem to have exceeded 5% of rental income, a sum much less than that spent by English landlords but not untypical of Irish landlord expenditure in post-famine years.[88] Many landlords still spent much of their money on extravagant building schemes. Gosford Castle was built in the 1820s at a cost of £80,000 while the earl of Kingston lavished £200,000 on building Mitchelstown Castle in the same period.[89] The most radical improvements took place in cases where estates previously held in rundale were altered into separate farms. On the Palmerstown estate in Co. Sligo an estimated £30,000 was spent on laying out new farms, providing access roads and building new isolated farmhouses to replace the nucleated settlements.[90] Many of these schemes proved difficult, expensive and not altogether successful. In order to provide the inhabitants of his Gweedore estate with access to the seashore and to bogland, Lord George Hill arranged the new holdings in long, very narrow, strips, often one mile in length, which were unlikely to be significantly more efficient than the holdings they replaced.[91] Often the fruits of such redistribution were destroyed when tenants insisted on subdividing the new holdings among their children contrary to estate regulations.

The degree to which estates were reorganised and farms reoriented in the pre-famine years is a matter of debate. Market conditions up to 1815 had undoubtedly favoured tillage, an activity which was both efficient and profitable on relatively small holdings and one which necessitated a large supply of labour. After 1815 the relative attractions of tillage receded and Ireland's traditional strength as a pastoral country reasserted itself. Contrary to common belief Mokyr asserts that there is 'no evidence of the relative price changes in favour of pastoral products after 1814'. However, Crotty argues that, at a time of falling prices, cattle which had lower input costs became more profitable, while the opening up of an export trade for live cattle provided a further boost.[92] At a time of uncertainty cattle farming may have appeared more secure than tillage; it was less vulnerable to the weather, while farmers who had accumulated money during the profitable war years had the wherewithal to stock holdings. Cattle farming also required larger farms and fewer workers.

The post-1815 period was marked by attempts at farm consolidation and by greater hostility to subdivision. William Greig's report on the Gosford estate was one of the first publications to note the evils of subdivision. In Co. Westmeath, whereas leases granted prior to 1815 contained little mention of subdivision, many of those granted in later years contained extraordinarily stringent penalties against this practice. One lease granted in 1827 on a holdings of four acres at a rent of £7, announced a penalty of £50, more than seven years' rent, in the event of subdivision.[93] Perhaps of greater interest, some leases also discouraged tillage by stipulating the maximum percentage of land to be ploughed and by enforcing stringent rotations. These measures may have prevented further subdivision from taking place, though in many cases subdivision was continuing on the eve of the famine. Measures to undo subdivision and to promote consolidation of farms were apparently less successful.

The evidence of the *Poor Inquiry* in the 1830s and of the *Devon Commission* of the 1840s, as analysed by Mokyr, suggests that consolidation was most common in Connaught and Munster, less frequent in Leinster and Ulster. Consolidation was effected by evicting existing tenants, by not renewing leases or by persuading tenants to leave by purchasing their interest. Eviction would appear to have been the most common method, except in Ulster, where purchase — the Ulster Custom — predominated. Many evictions were apparently motivated by a desire to consolidate, and eviction statistics therefore give some insight into this process. The *Devon Commission* records a total of 23,594 ejectments carried out by civil bill in the years 1839-43.[94] While not minimising the impact of eviction on the families concerned, the number remains relatively small when contrasted with the 769,000 odd farms of more than one acre in Ireland on the eve of the famine. Not all those ejected were permanently deprived of land: in the restriping of a rundale holding many were resettled. Landlords who owned vacant land on bogs or upland areas tended to resettle dispossessed tenants in these places—this was not uncommon in the western areas where waste land was relatively plentiful; others were offered emigration passages, while in Westmeath many used the compensation money to obtain a tenancy or conacre on nearby land, presumably not in the hands of an improving landlord.

While there was an undoubted urge to consolidate in the early nineteenth century it would not appear to have been fully realised. An examination of Westmeath, a county well-suited to cattle grazing, where the benefits of consolidation might have been greater than in other areas, concludes that there was 'no systematic consolidation before the famine, eviction or clearance being met with fierce opposition'.[95]

Agrarian violence was not a new phenomenon. Apart from an apparently isolated outburst by a group known as the Carders in the early eighteenth century, the first half of that century was extremely quiet. From 1760, when the first Whiteboy assaults manifested themselves in parts of Munster and south Leinster, there followed a regular series of outbreaks from varied secret societies with differing aims, regional locations and deriving their support from differing social groups.[96] Many had the purpose of protecting the interests of the poorer members of the community. Protests against either cost of or access to potato ground, enclosure of communal grazing land, hiring of migrant labourers at the expense of natives, the burden of protestant tithes or catholic marriage and baptism dues were among the innumerable grievances cited. The level of violence was high in the early nineteenth century. On the whole it correlated with times of agrarian depression;[97] it was apparently showing a steady upward curve[98] and, if we exclude the land war, it was higher than at any time in the post-famine period. During the late 1820s and early 1830s much of it related to the tithe war, a protest against the 1823 Tithe Composition Act and the ending of the exemption of grassland from tithes, changes which hit the middling and larger farmer, though benefiting the labourers and smallholder. This agitation drew in many larger farmers in Munster and south Leinster, and though it had some links with the secret societies there was little direct connection.[99]

While there remains considerable debate as to the underlying factors behind most agrarian violence, land would appear to play a predominant role and conflict frequently reflected differences between what E. P. Thompson has termed 'the moral economy of the poor'[100] and the wishes of thrusting, modernising landlords and farmers. In a survey of peasant assassinations in Co. Tipperary, Beames discovered that the majority of victims were new improving landlords, often catholics, some of them supporters of Daniel O Connell, frequently ex-businessmen who had bought estates and were determined to modernise them, or alternatively large improving tenant farmers who rented holdings which had been consolidated or transformed into cattle farms.[101] Mokyr's analysis of evidence to the *Devon Commission* noted that a majority of witnesses attributed agrarian outrages to evictions, which Mokyr believed were due to a desire to consolidate. Comparing evidence on the prevalence of consolidation from the *Poor Inquiry* of the 1830s with the *Devon Commission* of almost a decade later, he concluded that 'consolidation was slowed down considerably and in some places stopped altogether by violence, landlords' fear of violence, or by the landlords' compassion for the tenants who would be dispossessed'.[102] Lee has made a detailed analysis of agrarian outrage in the first five months of 1846, 'almost the last possible moment before the impact of the famine', concentrating on six west-midland counties — Limerick, Clare, Tipperary, Longford, Roscommon and Leitrim — an area accounting for 60% of agrarian crime though only containing 18% of Irish population. He discovered that the largest category of crime concerned disputes over conacre rented by labourers from farmers and he believes that farmer-labourer relations were involved in the majority of other disputes also.[103] Early 1846 may however be too late to avoid famine influences, though Lee's emphasis on conflict over conacre receives some support from Kenny's study of Westmeath which concluded that 'violence connected with conacre formed a considerable proportion of the general agrarian violence of the period'[104] and documented cases of conacre being granted or continued following threats or intimidation. Finally, in a study restricted to one extremely violent parish in Co. Leitrim, David Fitzpatrick also highlights the importance of land disputes, many of them intra-family. In several instances he documents violence perpetrated by an expanding modernising farmer against a relative occupying part of the family farm, his presence denying the expanding farmer access to this land.[105] All these studies appear, despite their differences, to contain one common theme, land pressure coupled with either a desire for or resistance to change.

Changes in the Irish linen industry also adversely affected the livelihood of many rural households. The introduction of machine spinning took place initially in the cotton industry, but by the second decade of the nineteenth century machine-spun linen yarn was being imported into Ireland. Its spread was limited by the low price of hand-spinning, but already by 1811 it was estimated that the balance of price advantage lay with the machine product.[106] The introduction of machine spinning meant a gradual ending of the earning possibilities of countless rural women who had earned small sums from 1/6 to 3/- per week, money which had frequently paid the rent and permitted a somewhat better lifestyle. Fewer yarn buyers came to the local markets and prices for yarn declined. In June 1816 the *Freeman's Journal* reported

> Scarcely any buyers attended Mullingar market and yarn fair on Monday 24th. The highest price for the best yarn did not exceed 1/- per lb. which at former fairs fetched from 1/8 to 2/-.[107]

There was still a market for fine yarns but this tended to be produced in the linen heartland of east Ulster and this was gradually undermined by the introduction of wet-spinning in the mid 1820s.

The timing of this collapse varied in different areas. In Mayo it would appear to have occurred towards the close of the 1820s.[108] The loss of income from yarn sales removed an important resource for many families. The shift to machine-produced yarn also affected weavers as weaving became centred in towns close to yarn supplies, and the number of independent rural weavers declined. The days of the farmer-weaver were numbered, though many continued to produce cloth for family and local consumption. In Erris, many redundant linen weavers switched to weaving wool. The market for their products was, however, limited to domestic and local consumption. Even this market was under threat as the spread of factory-produced cotton and woollen textiles provided lighter, more attractive cloths which were much in demand.

Precisely how households adapted to these circumstances remains unclear. Small holdings which had been rented as part industrial, part agricultural holdings were now reduced to depending exclusively on farming. Many Ulster women switched from spinning to embroidery.[109] Other peripheral areas developed alternative cash incomes: rabbit warrening, illicit distillation, kelp making, sale of seaweed for manure, were among the options.[110] Egg exports from Westport, Co. Mayo, rose rapidly in this period; for many households eggs replaced yarn as the major cash income, while migratory labour to England and Scotland also showed a sharp increase. Rising provision exports from the west may reflect both the opening up of some areas through road-building and the need to find a cash alternative. Ulster workers migrated to become factory spinners with men-folk employed as employee weavers. Others emigrated.

The Standard of Living in Pre-Famine Ireland

There exists a voluminous literature concerning changes in the standard of living in Britain during the late eighteenth and early nineteenth centuries. The topic cannot be debated with the same precision in Ireland because of a lack of statistical data. The period from 1815 to the famine was one of economic transition. Landlords and larger farmers faced problems but difficulties were undoubtedly greatest for the rural poor: smallholders, those dependent on domestic textiles, cottiers and unbound labourers. The Irish population was rising by approximately one per cent per annum — though the rise in the working age-group was somewhat less because of emigration. Irish national income would have needed to rise by a corresponding amount to prevent a fall in income per capita. Even if it did, there is no guarantee that the increased income would not accrue to the larger farmer at the expense of the cottiers and labourers.

The *Poor Inquiry* of the 1830s was decidedly of the opinion that conditions had deteriorated. They based this assertion heavily on comments made by the English agriculturist Arthur Young on conditions at the time of his visit to Ireland in the 1770s, as compared with their contemporary evidence 'that the peasantry were far better off, at the time of his visit, than they are at present'. They alleged an increased dietary dependence on the potato and 'the more frequent prevalence of fevers and famines'.[111] The latter point will be examined at a later stage. However, evidence of greater dependence on potatoes cannot be taken conclusively as indicating dire poverty. An adequate quantity of potatoes with small supplements provided a balanced diet. Mokyr has argued that the Irish liked eating potatoes and that this is confirmed by the loyalty to the potato diet among Irish workers in Britain, even when they received higher wages.[112] The overall impression of falling living standards is somewhat contradicted by the *Poor Inquiry's* comments of some 'little improvement' in the quality of clothing and cabins and the fact that, as they stated, 'the increase of shopkeepers and of goods at fairs is observed everywhere and they cannot sell without customers'.[113]

The majority of witnesses questioned by the *Poor Inquiry* when asked whether conditions had deteriorated, improved or remained static for the poorer classes since 1815, plumped for deterioration. While Co. Mayo apparently showed the greatest degree of pessimism, in provincial terms Ulster replies indicated the greatest decline. The Mayo pessimism contrasted with a greater degree of optimism in Galway and Leitrim. Munster and Leinster, though also choosing deterioration, were decidedly less pessimistic. As Mokyr suggests, the results correlate significantly with areas of domestic industry and would seem to reflect industrial rather than agricultural change[114]

Other indicators remain sketchy and must be treated with caution. The apparent stagnation of Irish butter exports from the 1820s may suggest that cottiers were finding it increasingly difficult to rent grass for a cow. Many had done so in the past, consuming the buttermilk at home and earning a valuable cash income from butter sales. The increasing tendency for farmers to insist on renting already manured conacre to labourers and charging a correspondingly higher rent also suggests a lack of cows among labourers with consequent lack of manure.[115] Analysis of possible changes in conacre rents and labourers' wages is fraught with difficulty. Examining the available figures for Co. Westmeath, Kenny discovered that, in many instances, higher wages were cancelled out by a correspondingly higher rent charged for a cabin. His returns from some landlords' wage books suggest money wages remaining stationary in the years from the 1820s to the famine,[116] a time when there was some fall in the overall price level.

Perhaps the greatest problem concerns the number of days worked by the average labourer. The *Poor Inquiry Report* was convinced that Ireland of the 1830s was characterised by a considerable degree of underemployment. In their third report they estimated that the number of people 'out of work and in distress for thirty weeks of the year' would amount to 585,000 people. These were estimated to have 1.8m. dependents, leaving the total number in distress for thirty weeks annually at 2,385,000. This statistic has been used to considerable effect to indicate the degree of acute distress prevailing in Ireland during the years leading up to the famine. We can only say that if these figures were true, mass mortality and probable population decline would have strongly prevailed during the mid 1830s if not before. The data was subjected to critical analysis by a contemporary who noted that the average figure for Mayo labourers' employment was based on returns from two parishes in the west of the county. For one parish, Kilgeever, a mere thirty-six days employment for labourers in the year was indicated, but this ignored the findings of the 1831 census that there were only eight landless labourers in the parish; in the other, Aughavale, where returns suggested an average of one hundred days employment, the 1831 census revealed not one family dependent totally on hire for its subsistence. Returns of days worked by labourers for the west of Ireland can be generally discarded as there were few genuine labourers in that area. The majority of the population consisted of small, often very small farmers or landholders; the large tillage farms were few in number, hence the limited demand for hired labour. Kenny's returns from landlord accounts in Westmeath suggest that cottiers were employed for 230-260 days, virtually full employment. The *Poor Inquiry* used a figure of ninety days for that county.[117]

An important matter in the 'standard of living' debate is access to conacre or potato ground. Most labourers depended on growing their own food; in many cases they could derive some cash income from their plot by fattening a pig. There is fragmentary evidence, from agrarian unrest for example, that some labourers were being denied conacre, but whether it was widespread we cannot say. The evidence of the *Poor Inquiry* suggests that rural misery was greater in Leinster than in the west of Ireland — though the latter area suffered considerably in years of potato failure, because Leinster proprietors had been more successful at displacing cottier-labourers, whereas in the west virtually all families held land.[118]

Access to land by labourers was undoubtedly vital. While unemployment undoubtedly existed in pre-famine Ireland it was primarily seasonal, reflecting the rhythms of the agricultural calendar. Labourers with conacre could balance periods of slack working for farmers or landlords with days spent cultivating their own holdings. Days not spent working for hire were therefore not necessarily spent in unemployment but in providing subsistence fuel or food. A rising population and the displacement of former textile workers probably meant greater competition for the paid agricultural work available and this may have resulted in lower wages or fewer working days. This, however, was partly counteracted by the opening of cheap steamship passages to Britain and the growth of cross-channel migratory labourers. The fact that women and children became involved in agricultural work at peak times to a greater extent than in post-famine times also suggests that virtually the whole of the labour force was required at such times.

Despite some efforts at restructuring, pre-famine agriculture remained predominantly concentrated on tillage and hence continued to require a large labour force. O Grada's figures, which show Irish agricultural output in 1854 falling 11-14% below its pre-famine level and the proportion derived from labour-intensive tillage falling from two-thirds to one-half, suggest that the pre-famine labourers were not altogether redundant. Irish agriculture in the 1850s could not equal its pre-famine output nor produce the same volume of labour-intensive tillage because it was operating with a significantly reduced workforce.[119]

Pre-Famine Demographic Adjustment

The post-war years gave rise to economic difficulties which were obvious to some sections of the Irish population. One of the interesting questions is the extent to which the Irish population responded to these circumstances. A significant critical debate exists as to whether the Irish population increase had begun to slow down before the famine. Analysis of this point rests to a considerable extent on how one interprets Irish demographic behaviour. Connell rested much of his analysis of marriage on the fact that misery provoked the population to marry early.

> In the late eighteenth and early nineteenth centuries it is clear that the Irish were insistently urged and tempted to marry early: the wretchedness of their living conditions, their improvident temperament, the unattractiveness of remaining single, perhaps the persuasion of their spiritual leaders, all acted in this direction.[120]

If one accepts Connell's premise, the most difficult years should have led to booming marriages; however evidence suggests the contrary. In the remote parish of Schull in West Cork, the catholic marriage register which recorded 71 marriages in 1814 dipped sharply to 44 and 45 in the famine years of 1816 and 1817. The next famine of 1822 showed marriages falling from 45 in 1820 to a mere 9, recovering to 41 in 1823.[121] The 1841 census suggests that the Irish marriage age may have been rising in the 1830s, while evidence from the Rotunda hospital records indicates that the age of mothers at the birth of their first child rose between 1811 and 1840 by 1.5 years.[122] Dublin cannot be taken as typical of Ireland as a whole; however, recent work by Boyle and O Grada, which employs complex statistical techniques, leads to the unequivocal result that Irish birth rates were dropping in the twenty years before the famine, a decline which seems partly attributable to a falling marriage rate.[123]

The most conclusive change in Irish demographic behaviour in the thirty years prior to the famine is the sharp and steady rise in emigration. Irish emigration to North America, especially among the Scots-Ulster community, had been a feature of eighteenth century life, though the numbers leaving were small. In the year 1795 there were only 44,000 Irish-born in the United States. The Napoleonic war artificially depressed emigration opportunities, not just from Ireland, but from Europe. The famine, or near-famine of 1816-17, however, coupled with an end to wartime difficulties, led to a major upsurge in numbers leaving Europe.[124] In the year 1818, 20,000 emigrated from Ireland and Adams, the authority on pre-famine emigration, sees these years as 'inaugurating a new trend',—the time when the 'true emigration trade' was established and the beginnings of emigration among the poor.[125] Thereafter, emigration fluctuated, though with a long-term upward trend. The early 1820s were a time of low emigration to the United States, but there was a considerable emigration into Britain, particularly Scotland. The financial crisis of 1826 caused a shift from British to trans-Atlantic emigration. In 1827 the official emigration total to North America reached 20,000—the true figure may have been 30,000; in 1831-2 more than 65,000 emigrated while no year after 1835 recorded a figure of less than 30,000. Irish emigration rose sharply in the early 1840s despite a serious depression in the U.S. and in 1842 over 100,000 left Ireland for North America.[126] During the thirty years 1815-45, approximately 2.5m. people left Europe for North America; of these Ireland contributed approximately one-third, ten times her population share.[127]

The rise in Irish trans-Atlantic emigration reflects a growing awareness of opportunities in North America, pessimism at Irish economic prospects plus the falling cost of emigration. Ships carrying cargoes of timber, fish, cotton and tobacco from North America to Britain, which had hitherto made the return journey without cargo, began to carry emigrants, bringing increased competition and lower prices. Cheaper passages, where emigrants provided their own food, also cut the cost as did the opening of cheaper routes to Quebec, New Brunswick and Newfoundland from where emigrants travelled by foot or by local transport to the U.S. In 1817, while the minimum price of a passage to the U.S. was ten guineas, it was possible to travel to New Brunswick for half that amount. As English shipowners became aware of the commercial possibilities Liverpool became the cheapest port of embarkation. By 1831 it was possible to travel from Newry to Liverpool and thence to New York for a mere £3.[128]

Even these prices would have been beyond the means of many. Pre-paid passages were provided by some landlords; tenants used the money awarded in compensation for eviction to emigrate,[129] while pre-paid passages and emigrants remittances, so much a feature of post-famine emigration, began to emerge. One-third of all passages handled by one Belfast shipping agent in 1834 were pre-paid in the U.S.[130]

Emigration to Britain was much less expensive and the few shillings required were apparently within the means of Mayo migratory labourers. Emigration to Britain is more difficult to document because of the lack of immigration records between Britain and Ireland. It fluctuated in accordance with periods of hardship and prosperity in the two countries, while the inflow shifted between one destination and another depending on the progress of the British industrial revolution.

The overwhelming majority of early emigrants were from Ulster, and initially they were disproportionately of Scots presbyterian stock. Unlike Irishmen of other areas, Ulster men and women of Scots descent had a tradition of emigration to North America; some presumably retained family ties with earlier emigrants. Their departure was triggered by the deterioration in the linen industry. Areas primarily dependent on spinning initiated the migration as they were the first to feel competitive pressure. Emigration lists for the years 1830-6 reveal that almost 80% of Irish emigrants to the U.S. came from Ulster. In addition to emigrating to the U.S. Ulster families also moved in significant numbers to Scotland or the north of England, particularly to textile areas. Mill owners from Dundee and Aberdeen advertised in the north of Ireland for weavers and spinners.[131] In Dundee over one-third of Irish emigrants listing a county of birth in the 1851 census came from Cavan and Monaghan, 20% from Leitrim, Fermanagh and Sligo, 15% from Donegal, Tyrone, Derry and 12% from Kings Co. In Paisley almost 70% came from Derry and Donegal.[132] The appearance of Sligo and Leitrim in these emigration figures reflects their position as part of the wider Ulster economic belt — particularly the linen belt. Sligo was the only non-Ulster county to supply a significant number of U.S. emigrants in the mid-1830s.[133] Outside of Ulster and its immediate hinterland, some other areas of early emigration were to be found in Leinster. Dublin, Carlow, King's, Queen's, Wexford had a significant volume of early emigration. Munster emigrants tended initially to go to Britain rather than North America, though the traditional Waterford-Newfoundland fishing ties brought a sizeable Waterford emigration to that area.[134]

The New York emigrant statistics reveal that, in the period 1820-34, Ulster and Leinster had almost equal shares, both accounting for almost 80% of emigrants whereas Connaught had a mere 6.7%. In the decade before the famine, however, the Connaught share almost doubled and it doubled again during the famine years. Emigration from the west therefore shows a steady rise, though it might be desirable to distinguish north Connaught from the remainder of the province.[135]

The occupational background of these early emigrants has long been a subject of comment and Adams infers that they were intellectually, financially and characterwise superior to their successors. In 1818 the *Dublin Evening Post* lamented

> It is a melancholy thing that emigration is necessarily restricted to the class immediately above the labouring order, who cannot raise the money to pay their passage.[136]

Artisans were heavily over-represented among those leaving relative to the population as a whole, though many, particularly the textile workers, possessed redundant skills. The largest single category were either labourers or servants. Farmers were relatively more common than in post-famine years. Some may have been evicted, others, particularly in Ulster, sold their interest and left. The belief that this pioneering emigrant populaton was an elite group is difficult to prove. The labourers and servants who predominated were not in that category, while analysis of emigrant ages suggests that emigrants were even more prone to age-heaping, that is to record their age in round numbers, 20, 30 etc. than the population as a whole, a practice which is deemed to indicate that they were less numerate, and probably less literate than the population as a whole.

Family emigrant groups were more common than in later times, so in consequence was the emigration of young children and older adults, though young adults predominated. Many emigrants travelled alone, men more frequently than women, who initially emigrated in family units. In time the number of unaccompanied women emigrants rose sharply so that in the post-famine period female emigration equalled that of men.[137] Women constituted a much higher proportion of emigrants to Britain, partly because of heavy Irish family emigration to new textile towns, perhaps because emigration to Britain was seen as cheaper and less hazardous for women and because Irish women with spinning skills were confident of employment in Britain.[138]

Emigration was the most obvious demographic reaction to the difficult economic circumstances in pre famine decades. Among the early emigrants the poorest parts of Ireland were undoubtedly underrepresented. This may be due to the cost of travelling, lack of information as to opportunities abroad, the distance and cost of getting to a boat, or the handicap of the Irish language. In Ulster emigration was low among the Irish speakers of the glens of Antrim and the mountainous parts of Tyrone and Derry.[139] Emigration undoubtedly made a contribution to reducing the rate of population increase in early nineteenth century Ulster, so that by the famine Ulster's population growth was the slowest in Ireland. It did not reduce pressure on land to any marked degree. In 1833 the *Londonderry Journal* wrote

> It is remarkable that the greater periodical emigrations from this district which have taken place have had no perceptible influence — indeed we are sure they have had none whatever, on rent or wages. New tenants rapidly fill up the vacancies caused by emigration and they continue, or at least they make an effort to pay the old rents by living more miserably than their predecessors would submit to.[140]

A Demographic Crisis in Pre-Famine Ireland?

One of the major topics of concern in the pre-famine economy is the extent to which the Irish population had reached the physical capacity of the Irish economy. This is suggested by K. H. Connell in his account of pre-famine disease and famines which is heavily dependent on the account given by Sir William Wilde in the 1851 census.

> For the seventy years before 1815 Wilde records one occasion on which nearly half of the crop (potatoes) was destroyed, three 'failures' and four partial failures. In the following thirty years he lists four major and eleven partial failures — in all as many bad years as good.[141]

Connell notes the limitation of Wilde's analysis, notably 'his reticence on the sources from which he derived his information', but adds

> no accounts have come to light, save for the years 1800 and 1801, of serious deficiencies in the first seventy years: nor for these years, with the added exception of 1771, are there records of fever epidemics on the scale that characteristically accompanied the later potato failures. There is, on the other hand, a mass of evidence bearing out Wilde's description of recurring and major deficiencies in the yield of the potato after 1815.[142]

The years 1816-17 were highlighted in this account as the first of the major years of crop failure. In fact there were also food difficulties in 1800-01 and 1813-14. However 1816-17 was a time of considerable scarcity throughout most of the northern hemisphere. This crisis was due to the explosion of the volcano of Tomboro on the Indian Ocean island of Sumbawa in 1815, which resulted in freakishly cold weather conditions. It has been dubbed by one historian, 'the last great subsistence crisis of the western world' — a title more appropriate to the Irish famine of the 1840s — and it resulted in a sharp increase in mortality in many parts of Europe. The Swiss death rate in 1817 was 56% above its 1815 level; that in Lombardy rose by 39%; Tuscany by 68%, Austria by 78%. In Switzerland, Austria, northern Italy and southern Germany the high mortality wiped out the natural increase in population.[143] The only Irish figures for these years, those of the contemporary medical historians Barker and Cheyne, suggest that Irish deaths increased by 65,000[144] — proportionately a much smaller increase than in the countries mentioned above. While not denying that these were years of hardship, this suggests that Ireland was less vulnerable in this particular crisis than much of Europe.

Contemporary evidence suggests that the incidence of food scarcity was greatest in the west of Ireland, yet this is the area recording the greatest population increase in the years prior to the great famine. It is important not to take anecdotal statements concerning distress as indicating that conditions approaching those of the famine years existed in the preceding decades. At present there exists no evidence indicating an overall increase in the Irish death-rate and some tenuous evidence that infant mortality was falling. The worst mortality at this time, as in other countries, occurred in towns and cities, though mortality in rural areas was highest in Connaught and lowest in Ulster.[145]

An examination of pleas for relief from distress during the years 1815-45 reveals a concentration along the western seaboard from Donegal to Kerry with the greatest number in west Mayo — Connemara. In 1822 it was estimated that around 50% of the population of Cork, Kerry, Limerick, Tipperary, Clare, Galway, Mayo, Leitrim, Sligo and Roscommon were in distress, with the worst conditions being experienced in Connemara and Erris. In 1831 the worst distress was in Connemara, west Mayo, Donegal and Clare. The year 1835 produced a familiar list of Mayo, Galway, Clare, Donegal and Kerry with conditions most acute in Erris and Connemara. The year 1837 brought Donegal, Clare and west Cork to the fore; 1839, Galway, Kerry, west Cork, parts of Clare and Mayo. The year 1842, apparently the first year when counties outside this traditional western belt were affected, saw reported distress in Cos. Tyrone, Wicklow, Carlow, Queen's Co, Westmeath, and Cavan, in addition to western areas.[146]

These reports suggest a crisis in the economy of the west of Ireland, due presumably to the pressure of a rising population. Whether these crises were new or not, we cannot judge. It is possible that, following on the 1816 crisis and resultant relief efforts which were set in motion, elements of the Irish population began to seek outside assistance in circumstances which had previously been met by purely local means.

One possible reason why this recurrent distress did not manifest itself in increasing mortality is because the relief measures applied proved to be relatively effective. The first major outbreak of post-war distress took place in the years 1816-17 and this is notable because the man responsible for Irish relief policy was Irish chief secretary, Robert Peel, who was British prime minister on the eve of the great famine. Peel's approach was a highly pragmatic one and it shaped his perception of the Irish problem almost thirty years later. Distress in 1816 seemed limited in area. Peel sent representatives to Donegal to discover the exact situation there and in the light of reports of a scarcity of food for purchase permitted the buying of large quantities of oats to be shipped to the area and sold at low prices. This enterprise was not well organised; the quality of the grain was poor and there was some fraud in its distribution.[147] This to some extent deterred other efforts of this nature. When distress on a greater scale presented itself in the following year Peel responded by setting up a commission to administer relief. Some biscuit was sent to areas of scarcity but the principal relief mechanism was public works schemes which Peel insisted should be instituted as quickly as possible. Government aid tended to be doled out in proportion to local contributions; much emphasis was placed on the involvement of local committees in relief efforts, though the commissioners were urged to take the initiative in areas where there were no resident gentry. The distress of 1816-17 was characterised by considerable generosity on the part of local gentry.[148] Total expenditure by the central relief committee amounted to approximately £30,624[149] — a small sum compared with later famine relief. Meanwhile, in Westminster, a bill was introduced permitting the government to issue exchequer bills for public works in both Britain and Ireland and a sum of £250,000 was made available for Ireland.[150]

The next year of major scarcity was 1822 when rural unrest helped to focus attention on Ireland. On this occasion the methods adopted in 1817 were continued. A potato shortage coincided with a good grain harvest and the government bought some corn for distribution in the west. Commissioners were again established and they placed their major emphasis on long term improvements rather than short-term relief. Local relief committees were given a central role. Their existence was seen as proof of real want in a locality and government assistance was given only when local gentry had already made a contribution. Between May and August the commission doled out £221,437 to local groups. The poor employment act, passed in that year, provided a long-term system for famine relief, with a fund of £250,000 to be loaned for public works schemes. The primary emphasis was on improved communications. Many reports noted the difficulty of transporting foodstuffs to some of the most distressed localities. Emphasis was also placed on harbour and fishery development. Sir Richard Griffith, subsequently famous for his valuation of Ireland, worked on roads in the mountainous and remote areas of Tipperary, Limerick, Cork and Kerry, employing 7,000 people in Limerick for a seven-week period. The relief efforts inaugurated in 1822 proved to be of long-term benefit. The funds voted in that year were spent on several successive years, lasting 'almost up to the introduction of the Poor Law'.[151] In the process communications were improved considerably. Road works in the Cork-Kerry region aimed to reduce the round trip to Cork from a six day journey to one lasting two days.[152] In the neighbourhood of Schull some areas were opened up to wheeled vehicles for the first time. Several of the new roads in that area were routed through bogs; in the process the land was drained and new cultivatable land created. Road building relieved destitution and opened up new areas. These remote locations were seen as areas of 'asylum for Whiteboys, smugglers and robbers'.[153] Better communications also brought the forces of law and order.

The fever epidemic of 1817 also encouraged a wave of state medical assistance. Funds specifically devoted to fever relief were channelled to western counties in the autumn of 1817 and they continued until the year 1822.[154] This epidemic led to the establishment of a small ad hoc government committee while government fever inspectors were appointed to report on the various provinces. Special assistance was given for the establishment of fever hospitals and in 1820 a general board of health — to advise the government on various health matters — was appointed. Further powers were taken in 1832 when a cholera epidemic threatened.[155] By the beginning of the nineteenth century every county had an infirmary. In the years up to the famine a system of out-patient dispensaries catering for those living at some distance from the infirmaries was instituted. We shall not pause to consider the effectiveness of the health-care offered; what must, however, be noted is the not inconsiderable state finances involved, though most infirmaries and fever hospitals drew from a combination of public and private sources.[156] Central government involvement in health and relief works in Ireland was far in excess of that in Britain at the time, giving some considerable credence to Prof. McDonagh's view of nineteenth century Ireland as an 'administrative laboratory' for English civil servants.[157]

Considerable though the government efforts were, private relief organisations were the mainstay of the poor during the years 'of scarcity, 1822, 1826 and 1831. Local relief committees borrowed government funds to supplement their own resources. In 1822 the plight of the peasantry of the west of Ireland roused considerable concern among English philanthropic interests and a committee of businessmen known as the London Tavern Committee raised a total of over £311,000. Their aid, like that of the government, was given to supplement local contributions. The funds were used to finance public works, provide cheap food and seed potatoes and they were disbursed by local committees consisting of catholic and protestant clergymen and local gentry.[158] In 1831 substantial voluntary aid was still forthcoming from members of this committee. They eventually set up some loan funds in the west to advance small sums to local peasants to buy fishing equipment or agricultural necessities. Charitable funds were also forthcoming from the Dublin Mansion House Committee.

From 1831, however, public sympathy with the plight of the Irish poor tended to diminish. The active involvement of local organisers dwindled and the importance of private subscriptions was reduced. Within Ireland some landlords apparently wearied of the continual calls on their resources at a time when they faced financial difficulties. The landlord class divided between those concerned citizens who attempted to help the peasantry and inactive, often absentee, landlords who were seen as shirking their responsibilities.

Rising sectarian tensions increased the strains in local committees. Catholic and protestant were less likely to act side by side following increasing catholic politicisation as a result of catholic emancipation and an upsurge of protestant proselytising efforts initiated by protestant clergymen described by one writer as 'zealous to the point of rashness'.[159] The main thrust of the protestant evangelising campaign was in the west and south-west of Ireland, precisely the areas most affected by distress and poverty. Some of the more militant evangelicals undoubtedly took advantage of poverty and distress to win converts, while any protestant clergyman who engaged in famine relief was liable to find himself charged with 'souperism' — attempting to win converts with material blandishments. Le Poer Trench, the evangelical archbishop of Tuam, who organised an apparently impartial relief committee during the famine of 1822, was accused by his rival, Dr. John McHale, of souperism.[160] The year 1822 marked the relative peak of English private contributions towards Irish distress: the proportion of total assistance which they provided was considerably greater than during the great famine. In 1845 at the beginning of the famine, Lord Monteagle recalled the work of the London Tavern Committee

> We adopted the principle as far as we could of giving our aid in furtherance of local efforts and through local bodies regularly constituted, responsible and rendering an account of their expenditure. At present, unfortunately, I anticipate no such effort of a private nature in England. Various causes, some rational, others unreasonable have diminished, if they have not totally extinguished the sympathy on which in 1822 we relied. I therefore feel that if an extreme case should render the interposition of other necessities, it must be public assistance alone that can be looked to.[161]

Irish landlords were increasingly held responsible for conditions which led to apparent near-famine in Ireland. English classical economists reserved their strongest strictures for Irish landlords,[162] while the belief that Irish property had a responsibility to support Irish poverty became common among both politicians and the general public alike. During the scarcity of 1831 the government publicly blamed the landlords for the conditions of the people and emphasised their duty to alleviate poverty.[163] Some support for these views comes from O'Neill's analysis of relief measures adopted during the years between 1815 and the famine. He concludes that

> Despite the exceptions the traditional picture of a landlord class showing disinterest in the sufferings of their tenantry is reinforced from a study of relief in this period.[164]

Government sympathy for Irish famine dwindled. In the difficult year 1837 special government relief was in short supply.[165]

Britain, however much she wished, could not ignore Irish poverty. Ireland was part of the union; there was a strong fear that England might be swamped by large-scale immigration of the Irish poor which would depress wage levels and living standards, intensify unemployment and pose an impossible burden for English poor relief, while English farmers felt that their market was being undermined by cheap Irish corn imports, produced by underpaid labour.[166]

British Government Policy Towards Ireland, 1815-45

Government proposals to resolve Irish poverty divided into three categories: public works, assisted emigration and the establishment of a poor law. Public works had been an integral part of ad hoc famine relief in Ireland from the second decade of the century, with the government favouring them over the direct provision of food in most circumstances. While the building and financing of local roads remained the responsibility of locally controlled grand juries, central funds advanced an estimated one million pounds for the building of roads, bridges, harbours and other forms of infrastructural expenditure between the years 1817 and 1831, most of the money going to remote and impoverished areas. Control of such expenditure until 1831 rested with a rather unwieldy group of unpaid commissioners. In 1831, perhaps because of official dissatisfaction — which led to an inquiry into the poor quality of roads built by the engineer Nimmo in Connemara during the 1820s — control was transferred to three full-time commissioners who became the reconstituted Irish Board of Works. The board disbursed a combination of loans and small grants to both individuals and to public bodies for various long-term improvements such as roads, harbours and bridge-building. In 1842 drainage and fisheries were added to their responsibilities.[167] Between 1831 and 1845 they advanced over one million pounds, £980,000 in loans and £125,000 in direct grants, much of it to grand juries.[168] Other government agencies examined the possibility of bog clearance and land improvement while fisheries received considerable attention. These measures were regarded as furthering long-term development so that the Irish economy would ultimately become self-sustaining. Similar views of the value of public works as a measure to relieve Irish poverty and promote economic development were advanced in the report of the *Irish Poor Inquiry* and the report of the *Railway Commissioners*.

The latter, set up under the chairmanship of the under-secretary for Ireland, proposed that two major railway lines — one running through the north, the other through the south of the country — be built, either by willing capitalists, or, failing them, by private enterprise assisted by low-interest state loans.[168] Railway construction was seen, not only as affording much needed employment but as opening up the interior of the country to greater commercialisation and so encouraging the development of more intensive agricultural production with consequent employment benefits.[169] These proposals were aired on various occasions in parliament; abortive railway bills were introduced, the most famous being Bentinck's attempt to meet some of the distress of the great famine by launching such a proposal.[170]

The most comprehensive attempt to tackle Irish poverty through state investment was the report of the *Poor Inquiry* chaired by Richard Whatley, TCD economist and archbishop of Dublin. This report estimated that 2,385,000 people, 585,000 of them able-bodied, were in need of assistance. The key proposal was that

> enactments calculated to promote the improvement of the country, and so to extend the demand for free and profitable labour should make essential parts of any law for ameliorating the conditions of the poor.

To this end they proposed the establishment of a Board of Improvement charged with clearing wastelands and an expanded Board of Works to provide roads and drainage in such newly-cleared lands. The removal of insanitary cabins by landlords, agricultural model schools and the establishment of a fiscal board to regulate the expenditure were also suggested, while mention was made of the need to encourage fishery development.[171] These far-reaching proposals had little prospect of acceptance in the economic climate of England in the 1830s. However, it can be argued that in a diluted form the attempted development of Ireland through public works was already being undertaken during the pre-famine years. The fact that prior to 1846 there is no evidence of exceptionally high mortality during years of distress suggests that public works *may* have prevented catastrophic loss of life, but there is no evidence that they brought long-term progress. One authority, Collison Black states that

> The coming of the Famine was at once a proof of the failure of the system of public works so far established to resolve the Irish economic crisis.[172]

Assisted emigration was another possible solution which received considerable attention in the pre-famine decades as it became obvious that the level of spontaneous emigration was rising sharply. Landlord assistance to emigrants also increased. In evidence collected by the *Poor Inquiry* from 363 parishes, 47 reported direct landlord-assisted emigration, while 23 others reported emigration assisted by public subscription.[173] Two parliamentary select committees in 1826 and 1827 examined the arguments both for and against emigration and ended by endorsing a large-scale plan for state-aided emigration.[174] The fear of Irish emigration to England caused many to advocate emigration to North America as more desirable. However, state-aided emigration schemes foundered because of the high costs involved. The costs in pilot emigration schemes organised to Canada were exceptionally high because they included, not only the cost of passage, but the cost of establishing the emigrants in homes and occupations in the new world.[175] The *Poor Inquiry* did not regard emigration as the major remedy for Irish poverty, though they recommended that all those wishing to emigrate 'should be furnished with the means of doing so in safety'.[176]

Failing public works or emigration there remained the option of introducing a poor law. Ireland, unlike England, had not traditionally had a poor law, and the relief of the destitute, the crippled and all other categories in need had traditionally rested with the common population. However, Irish hospitality traditions, which guaranteed food and shelter to all strangers, had generally met the most urgent requirements. Hence to English eyes beggars abounded, often bringing in their wake fevers and epidemic diseases. During the late spring and early summer months, between the end of the old potato crop and the harvesting of the new, many labouring families went on the tramp begging for food. One west Cork labourer, fifty-year old Patrick Hegarty, told the *Poor Inquiry*

> I am fifty years old. I have a wife and five children, the eldest is only nine. I went to beg last summer; it was for the first time I had no employment. She went out every summer since. In the winter I used to gather twigs for making little baskets for gathering potatoes. The neighbours used give us potatoes in the plentiful season. I was obliged to go out myself last May; we had another young child and I went to carry it.[177]

The introduction of some form of poor law to Ireland was proposed on several occasions in the light of the scarcities of 1817 and following years. Such suggestions initially met with much hostility from English economists, who deplored the laxity of the English poor law and its encouragement of idleness and improvidence among the poor. In Ireland it was felt that a poor law would only serve to encourage even greater improvidence, perpetuating practices of subdivision, early marriages and large families. However, in the early 1830s the English poor law was subjected to major reform. The old practices of supplementing the wages of farm labourers during times of scarcity and granting outdoor relief to the able-bodied were curbed, in the teeth of much opposition, and the workhouse with its emphasis on 'lesser eligibility' and institutional regulation became the common method of poor relief. It was felt that these reforms would have the effect of improving the incentive to work and encouraging the mobility of labour from the relatively depressed agrarian areas of the south of England to the expanding areas of the north. In Ireland it was felt that, while any form of outdoor relief would prove prohibitively expensive, this argument would not necessarily apply to workhouses and that, while living conditions in the workhouse were unlikely to be more unpleasant than those in labourers' cabins, the institutional controls, strict regulation and segregation of families would prevent the population making excessive demands on the system. The introduction of some form of poor relief was seen as a necessary preliminary to abolishing the system of cottiers and extensive subdivision of farms and their replacement by a system of capitalist agriculture. It was felt that the Irish peasants clung to their potato patches as the only guarantee against destitution while the lack of a poor relief system deterred landlords from eviction.[178]

The introduction of the workhouse system to Ireland was opposed by a variety of interests. The *Poor Inquiry Commission* rejected this option, partly on the grounds of expense. They argued that there were 2,385,000 in poverty in Ireland: the cost of housing all these in workhouses would be prohibitive. Instead they recommended legal provision, financed by rates, to support the blind, idiots and such categories, comprehensive hospitals or home relief for the sick, and institutions to provide for deserted children, orphans, the aged and infirm and helpless widows.[179] They rejected the use of workhouses for the destitute able-bodied on the grounds that, whereas they had been introduced in England in order to force the poor to work rather than remain idle, 'in Ireland we see that the labouring class are eager for work, that work there is not for them and that they are therefore, and not from any fault of their own, in permanent want'.[180] Landlords also opposed the introduction of poor relief on the grounds of cost, while Daniel O'Connell viewed it as an alien institution from which Ireland might escape by repeal of the union.[181]

The British government rejected the recommendations of the *Poor Inquiry Commission* on the grounds that

> the suggestions in it were not of that simple and single nature as to allow them to be adopted without the caution which was recommended by the Commissioners themselves.[182]

They were more sympathetic to a report from George Cornwall Lewis, an Irish assistant commissioner, which urged the introduction of the workhouse system, a call which was endorsed by a report from George Nicholls, a member of the English poor law commission. Nicholls countered the prevailing tone of pessimism in the *Poor Inquiry* with the 'conviction that the condition of Ireland has, on the whole, during the last thirty years been progressively improving'.[183] He unhesitatingly recommended the workhouse system, countering the estimate of 2,385,000 in need of assistance with an alternative figure of 80,000. Both figures were probably correct. As Collison Black notes, while the *Poor Inquiry Commission* estimated the numbers in poverty at 2,385,000, Nicholls merely calculated the numbers in actual destitution.[184] It was feasible to provide workhouse accommodation for

80,000, but not for 2,385,000, and the workhouse system which was introduced into Ireland from 1840 was geared to a theoretical capacity of 100,000. It was only designed to deal with normal destitution, Nicholls specifically emphasising that 'the occurrence of a famine, if general, seems to be a contingency altogether above the powers of a Poor Law to provide for'.[185]

What was the probability in the late 1830s that Ireland would experience a major famine? This is an area where we must avoid post-hoc reasoning. The knowledge that a major famine did take place has undoubtedly distorted the analysis of men such as Wilde in the 1851 census and of many later writers. Pre-famine Ireland has generally been viewed as existing in a classic Malthusian trap with population increasing more rapidly than food supply and the so-called Malthusian solution emerging in the great famine. Malthus however, as Cormac O Grada has recently pointed out, said relatively little about Ireland and what he said was somewhat confused. Malthus can be read in several different ways. The malign version leads to a famine-type outcome, the benign version to demographic adjustment bringing about a decline in population growth through changes in marriage, reproductive patterns and emigration.[186] Joel Mokyr, using cross-section data for the 32 Irish counties in 1841, found no association between rural population density, the cultivated land-labour ratio and poverty. Mokyr's results mean, in his own words, that 'serious doubt has been cast on the simple and easy explanation which blames Irish poverty on excess population'.[187] However, a further conclusion that 'had there been no famine Ireland's population would have continued to grow like any other European country in the second half of the nineteenth century'[188] would seem to be an overstatement. Evidence that Irish population was reacting positively, if not to a Malthusian check, perhaps to difficult economic circumstances and a growing awareness of improved prospects overseas, emerges from the steadily rising level of pre-famine emigration and perhaps from the more tentative evidence of a rising marriage age and falling birth-rate. The rate of population increase after 1821 was considerably less than in earlier decades and while Ireland, in the absence of famine, was unlikely to have recorded static or falling population in 1851, as Carney's analysis of Trinity College estate population suggests,[189] a move towards long-term population stability seems not implausible. Whether this response should be termed Malthusian is rather questionable. The response came first from Ulster, the province which, because of a more diversified economy, appears to have been least affected by food scarcity. Reaction in areas such as the west was undoubtedly slower.

Famines are not caused by food scarcity alone. Nevertheless it is worth exploring whether food scarcity was a problem in pre-famine Ireland. The evidence which might favour this interpretation comes from the food shortages of the pre-famine years; yet there is equally persuasive, if less publicised, evidence of difficult years in the second half of the eighteenth century.[190] O Grada goes so far as to suggest that 'the most serious crises of the 1740-1800 period could have been *worse* than anything occurring between 1800 and the Great Famine'.[191] That there were cases of hunger and hunger-related disease in the decades prior to the famine is not in doubt. One account of famine distress in Derrybeg, Co. Donegal speaks of 'a great number of (his) people (are) swelling up in the most frightful manner', presumably a reference to hunger oedema and also writes of victims 'vomiting blood'.[192] However such occurrences were not sufficiently common to make any apparent impact on the natural increase of population. In many instances distress was deemed to be the result not of lack of food, but in Kerry in 1822 of a lack of money,[193] or in the words of a parliamentary inquiry into conditions in parts of the west in 1835, 'from want of employment rather than absolute scarcity'.[194] Many other complaints relate not to absolute scarcity but to the high prices being charged. Even in cases where food was deemed to be scarce this could reflect the fact that traders, realising that the area was impoverished, did not think it profitable to send in food.[195]

Deaths from starvation were apparently few, while evidence from the *Poor Inquiry* does not indicate any dramatic increase in the incidence of fever and other hunger-related diseases. The replies to questions about this vary considerably. Some, as in Frenchpark, Co. Roscommon, reply that fever was 'much more severe and varied than formerly', which is attributed to greater poverty, but many replies indicate the contrary. Millstreet, Co. Cork had not experienced serious fever since 1822, and in Ballyconnell, Co. Cavan, the last major epidemic took place in 1824, though there was 'a great deal of low fever from time to time'.[196] The replies do not indicate that any particular area was more affected by fever than others and certainly cannot be used to suggest that the incidence of fever was rising sharply a decade before the famine.

Sections of the pre-famine population, notably the labourers, suffered from food scarcity on occasion, primarily in the early summer. Replies to the *Poor Inquiry* suggest that for many there was a gap between the consumption of the old potatoes and the harvesting of the new season's crop; a gap which varied between one week, or virtually no gap, to a fairly normal one month and as much as three months in years of exceptionally bad weather.[197] This could be taken as indicating that Irish food supplies were inadequate to feed the population, but the matter is more complicated. Bourke suggests that an estimated third of the pre-famine potato crop in a normal year went to feed animals, mainly pigs and cattle.[198] This provided a safety barrier for humans. In years of scarcity the animals, especially the pigs, went short and pig numbers fell. In normal, even in most below-normal years, the Irish potato crop was more than adequate to feed the population. The problem would appear to be one of reliability and storage. Mokyr, using French early nineteenth century statistics, in the absence of Irish figures, has argued that potatoes were less reliable than grain, but it seems invalid to use French data to answer the question for Ireland which has a much wetter climate, making grain harvests more vulnerable than in the case of France.[199] The storage problem is something of a paradox, as the South American Indians had traditionally stored potatoes for long periods.[200] In Ireland, however, all witness to the *Poor Inquiry* concur in lamenting the inability to carry over surplus potatoes from one year to another and some ingenious solutions which would involve making starch or a farinaceous substance from surplus potatoes were advanced.[201] The answer may lie in the fact that the Irish traditionally ate potatoes primarily in the winter months and thought of them as a winter food. L. M. Cullen has argued that the complete dependence on the potato developed at a relatively late stage, the early nineteenth century.[202] It this is so, the early summer potato scarcity among labourers and smallholders reflects the imperfect adjustment to seeing the potato as a year-round food. The early summer was regarded as the 'meal months': the term is undoubtedly significant.

When examined more closely the seasonal scarcities reflect more of an economic problem, a lack of money and employment, than crude shortage of food. The fact that potatoes were exhausted at a time, June and July, when agricultural work was scarce—haymaking appears to have been much less important than later in the century— meant that labourers were not in a position to earn much money and were also less likely to be fed by the farmer. Few labourers had the resources to save money for these difficult months. The normal response was recourse to credit at what can only be termed usurious rates. Thus two Galway witnesses explained

> A man who bears a good character and is no drunkard will get credit but he must pay well for it. When the price of meal is 10/- he must by getting three months time pay 16/-.

> I never knew a labourer who was able to lay anything by that was worth speaking of. The majority of them live in the greatest privation and are supported by pledging and promising, and when they get employment, paying.[203]

Credit was provided by hucksters, or in the terminology of the Church of Ireland archbishop of Tuam, 'scullogues' — farmers who had saved money.[204] Such loans were repaid after the harvest work had been completed, or when a migrant returned from working in England or in the east of Ireland. Considerable priority was given to repaying such loans in order to ensure that credit would be renewed. The food purchased on credit was generally meal, but could also be potatoes, suggesting that mere scarcity of potatoes does not fully account for shortages. Many of the transactions, either in buying food or borrowing money, took place between farmers and labourers, though witnesses to the *Poor Inquiry* suggested that credit was becoming more difficult to obtain. Witnesses from Co. Carlow, Co. Cavan and other parts testified to a declining availability of credit since labourers were finding it more difficult to repay loans because of a lack of employment. Credit was frequently only provided if they had some resources such as a plot of land, or if they could get a person of substance to sign their promissory note. Those who could not obtain credit were reduced to begging and all accounts suggest that begging, particularly by women and children, was rife in pre-famine Ireland. Alms and assistance, particularly food, were relatively generously disbursed.

All this suggests that the principal pre-famine problem was not a lack of food, but of the resources, particularly money, to command it. Problems could be compounded by the fact that potatoes were extremely bulky and it was prohibitively expensive to transport them over long distances so that there were problems in alleviating local shortages. Many of the most distressed areas were geographically remote and poorly served, at least in 1815, with roads. Relief works in the succeeding years did much to open up communications, and this provided a lucrative market for those with food surpluses. A witness to the *Poor Inquiry* remarked that 'latterly' meal was being shipped out of Kilgeever, Co. Mayo, making it more difficult for the poor to buy some 'at any rate'.[205] The problem of distress in pre-famine Ireland, and also during the famine years, cannot be simply explained in terms of the availability or shortage of food. Economic purchasing power, market forces, transport and communication, the very fabric of society, all play their part.

PART 2

THE FAMINE

Causes of Famine

'Natural factors cause crop failures, but human beings cause famines'. (William A. Dando, *The geography of famine* p. viii)

The blight, which first attacked the Irish potato crop in the autumn of 1845 introduced a new element into the history of Irish famine. The 1740-41 famine was caused by extremely harsh weather which prevented the peasants from getting the potatoes out of the ground. The blight introduced some novel and undesirable elements. While the probability of two exceptionally cold, or wet, or dry years succeeding one another is slight and the probability of similarly freakish weather conditions occurring for five consecutive seasons is minimal in Ireland, the blight could and did persist from one season to another remaining dormant in the soil through the winter months. In addition, the impact of disease was probably more immediate, more dramatic and more total than ravages caused by weather. Contemporaries invariably wrote about the suddenness with which the blight struck: fields which had been healthy and luxuriant one day, a mass of diseased plants the next. Land agent William Steuart Trench had planted potatoes on high land in King's Co.

> On August 6, 1846 — I shall not readily forget the day — I rode up as usual to my mountain property, and my feelings may be imagined when, before I saw the crop, I smelt the fearful stench, now so well known and recognised as the death sign of each field of potatoes. I was dismayed indeed, but I rode on; and as I wound down the newly engineered road, running through the heart of the farm, and which forms the regular approach to the steward's house, I could scarcely bear the fearful and strange smell, which came up so rank from the luxuriant crop then growing all around; no perceptible change, except the smell, had as yet come upon the apparent prosperity of the deceitfully luxuriant stalks, but the experience of the past few days taught me that all was gone, and the crop was utterly worthless. . . . It is enough to say that the luxuriant stalks soon withered, the leaves decayed, the disease extended

to the tubers, and the stench from the rotting of such an immense amount of rich vegetable matter became almost intolerable. I saw my splendid crop fast disappearing and melting away under this fatal disease.[1]

Blight is caused by *phythopthera infestans*, a fungus which multiplies in hot, damp weather and can be quickly disseminated by wind or mist. Rainwater carries the spores from the leaves of the potatoes to the roots and causes the tubers to become infected. A whole field could be destroyed in a matter of hours. The disease could survive in a dormant fashion through the winter months in partially diseased tubers, which might be planted as seed potatoes, allowing the fungus to spread devastation during the following season. The fungus apparently came to Europe from South America on boats carrying guano, the newly-popular fertiliser. In the year 1845 the Netherlands lost approximately two-thirds of its potatoes, Belgium a staggering seven-eighths. Matters improved relatively rapidly. In 1846 Belgium harvested two-thirds of its normal crop, the Netherlands one third. The severe drought of the late summer of 1846 had succeeded in killing the blight. Deaths rose in both countries, though by considerably less than in Ireland.[2]

From the continent the potato blight spread to England and by the summer of 1845 it had reached the Isle of Wight. By August 1845 blight was found everywhere in England except the northern area, and by September 13 the first sighting was reported in Ireland in the vicinity of Dublin. It was carried to Ireland by south-east winds which blew frequently, if untypically, during the late summer and early autumn of 1845.[3] On September 16 the constabulary was ordered to report weekly on blight damage in their area and by 16 October it had spread to seventeen counties.[4]

The incidence of blight in 1845 varied considerably between the different parts of Ireland. Using the constabulary reports we can gain an impression of the relative impact, though it must be noted that the figures used in Map 1 are undoubtedly an overestimate of the incidence. The most severely affected counties would appear to have been Waterford, Antrim, Monaghan, and Clare, while losses in the Dublin-Meath area and in Co. Down were high, as they were in the Limerick-Tipperary area and in Co. Roscommon and parts of Co. Galway. Losses in Mayo, however, were below average. The severity of the 1845 failure was reduced because the worst incidence was in the more prosperous eastern counties.[5] Its impact was also mitigated by the fact that the blight did not spread widely until October-November, by which time the early potatoes had been lifted, in a year

54 THE FAMINE

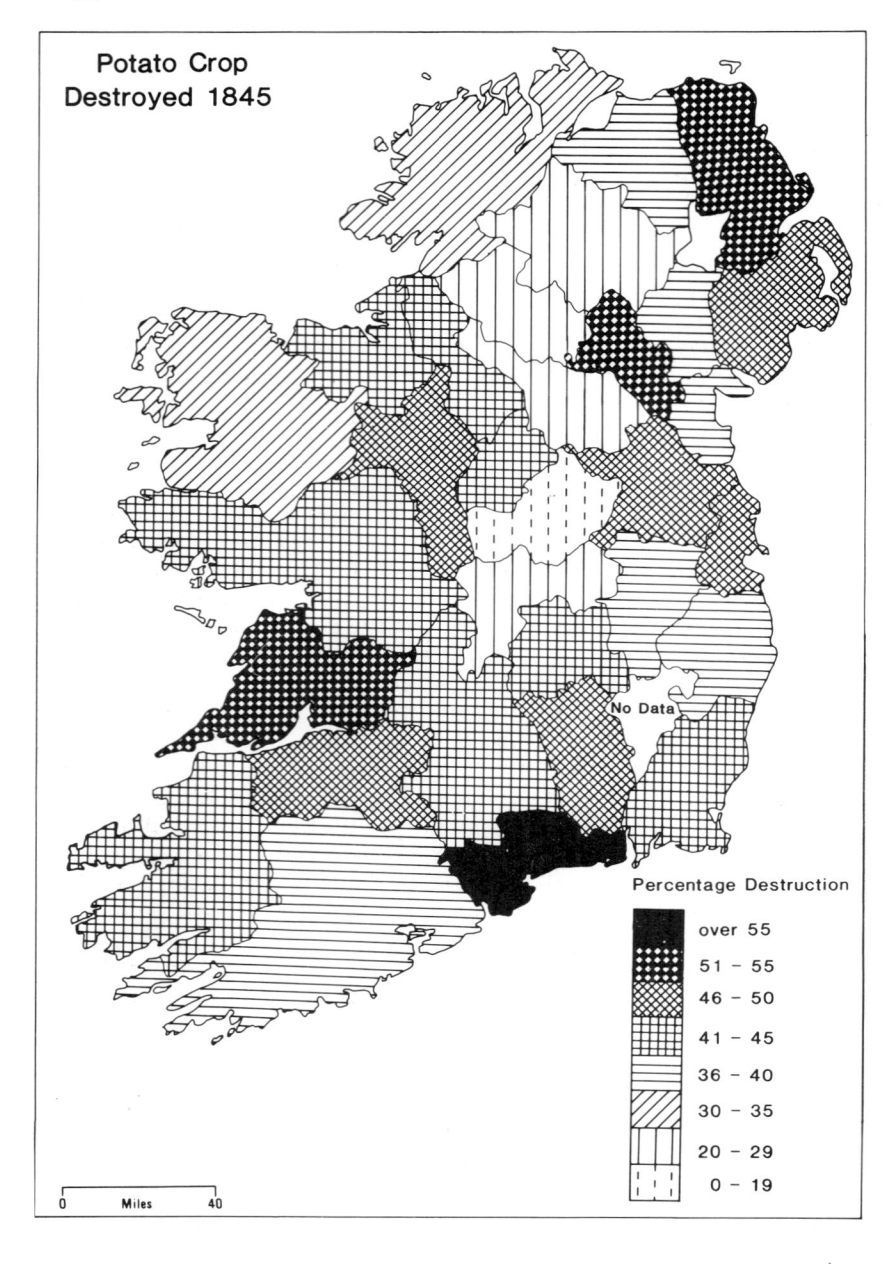

Potato Crop Destroyed 1845

Percentage Destruction

- over 55
- 51 – 55
- 46 – 50
- 41 – 45
- 36 – 40
- 30 – 35
- 20 – 29
- 0 – 19

No Data

0 Miles 40

when the early crop had been particularly prolific. Bourke estimates the total loss in 1845 at slightly less than one-third of the 1844 crop.[6] The real devastation came in 1846 and subsequent years.

The 1846 crop would have been smaller than usual, because of the disease affecting the main crop potatoes which meant that seed potato was both scarce and of uncertain quality. On this occasion disease struck much earlier than in 1845. Warm damp summer weather was ideally suited to the spread of blight and by August reports of devastation came from every part of the country.[7] Potato planting was later than in modern times and the new season's crop was generally not available until the end of July or beginning of August.[8] By early August virtually the whole crop was threatened, though some areas escaped more lightly than others. The district of the Maharees and Castlegregory to the north of the Dingle peninsula was said to have suffered only partial destruction.[9] Throughout the autumn and winter of 1846 there are reports of some potatoes coming to market in various areas and of children harvesting potatoes in the fields. However, the potatoes in question seem to have been small, immature and few in number. The combination of a lack of seed potatoes, though the Society of Friends supplied some, plus a belief by many experts that the Irish peasantry should be encouraged to concentrate on alternative crops such as turnips, combined with a shortage of field labour (see below) meant that the potato acreage planted in 1847 was extremely small though the yield was high and the crop virtually blight-free. The total crop, however, would seem to have been less than in the disease-ridden year of 1846. In 1847 the heaviest planting relative to 1845 would appear to have been maintained in counties such as Antrim, Armagh, Kerry, Queen's, Carlow, Kildare and Wicklow; the lowest relative to previous seasons in Mayo, Roscommon and Sligo. Clare and Galway were also well below the national average.[10] In 1848, a year of substantially greater planting, blight returned in high season, though in a somewhat patchy fashion. The average yield per acre was somewhat over half that achieved in 1847; but figures much in excess of that were achieved in Wicklow, Donegal, Fermanagh, Kerry, Wexford and Mayo; the lowest yields by far were in a belt of counties in the midlands, Cavan, Longford, Meath, Monaghan, Dublin, Westmeath and Kildare,[11] though these were not the counties which suffered most during 1848. The following year, 1849, with a potato acreage reduced from the 1848 level and a respectable yield, might be deemed the first year of post-famine normality, though the pre-famine potato acreage was never regained, nor indeed were pre-famine potato yields—partly because of blight, but also because of the demise of intensive agricultural practices.

POTATO CROP AT TIME OF FAMINE[12]

	Acres (000)	Yield per acre	Produce (000 tons)
1844	2,378	(6.25) est.	(14,862) est.
1845	2,516	(4.0) est.	(10,063) est.
1846	1,999	(1.5) est.	(2,999) est.
1847	284	7.2	2,046
1848	810	3.8	3,077
1849	719	5.6	4,024

A shortage of food alone does not account for famine, nor does it explain who the victims will be. The Indian economist, Sen, estimated that in the famine year of 1943 in Bengal the total food supply was only 5% less than its average level in the five preceding years and that food supplies were actually 13% greater than in the year 1941 when there was no famine.[13] In Ireland, however, food was genuinely scarce during the famine years. Bourke, working on an average consumption of twelve lbs. of potatoes per day per adult male cottier for 10½ months per year, estimated that a total of 7m. tons of potatoes were used each year for human food, with a further 2m. for seed and 5m. for animal food.[14] On the basis of these figures it could be argued that the 1845 crop, though reduced, offered enough food for human consumption and seed, though it was not necessarily in the hands of those who most needed it and was not evenly distributed throughout the country. By any standards the potato tonnages of 1846, 47 and 48 were totally inadequate to meet the needs of the population. The most important question, however, is whether other food resources in the country might have provided an adequate alternative.

On the eve of the famine Ireland exported a considerable amount of grain. Solar has estimated that the pre-famine food exports could feed an average of 1-1¼m. people at English standards of consumption. The continuing export of grain during the famine years is a topic which has given rise to considerable nationalist criticism. John Mitchel alleged that every ship bringing relief supplies of grain into Ireland during the famine was likely to meet six ships leaving the country laden with grain.[15] Bourke's figures suggest, however, that the grain exports of 1846 totalled approximately 285,000 tons, the food equivalent of slightly more than one million tons of potatoes, while the potato shortfall in that year was 'well over ten times that figure'. Imports during the ten months from September 1846 to June 1847 were about five times the volume of exports, totalling 659,000 tons, and on Bourke's estimates would have had the equivalent food value of approximately

2.5m. tons of potatoes, or one-quarter of what was needed. Total supplies of grain and potatoes were therefore inadequate; exports were much exceeded by imports, though food exports were concentrated in the autumn of 1846, imports in the period from December 1846 and the early months of 1847. Had the food exported during the autumn of 1846 been kept in Ireland it 'could have made an appreciable contribution to bridging the starvation gap between the destruction of the potato crop in August and the arrival of the first maize cargoes in the following winter'.[16]

In addition to grain exports, livestock exports also continued during the famine years.

	1846	1847	1848	1849[17]
Oxen bulls cows	186,483	189,960	196,042	201,811
Calves	6,363	9,992	7,086	9,831
Sheep, lambs	259,257	324,179	255,682	241,061
Swine	480,827	106,407	110,787	68,053

Cattle exports rose steadily during the famine years but pig exports fell sharply because pigs were fed on potatoes. Few peasant families could afford to eat any quantity of meat even in normal years; pork and bacon were the meats normally eaten, beef was too expensive. The substitution of beef for potatoes would have been financially impossible and limits on livestock exports, or on grain exports, would probably have been counterproductive. Attempts to keep the food in Ireland by legislative decree would not have ensured that the food so held would have reached those most in need, while such restrictions would have probably deterred food imports. Ireland was short of food during the famine years and needed all possible imports. In fact, demands for controls on exports of food were negligible during the famine years.[18]

In normal years most Irish families were virtually self-sufficient in potatoes and only a small proportion of the total crop entered into commercial trade. The failure of the potato crop not only robbed families of their dietary mainstay, it also forced the Irish population to buy the bulk of their food rather than producing it themselves. Food had now to be acquired through cash transactions on a hitherto unprecedented scale. This placed considerable pressure on the monetary resources of the Irish banking system. One of the first government initiatives was to arrange an adequate supply of silver coin throughout the country.[19] The food distribution system was also inadequate. It had hitherto coped primarily with food exports rather than imports and in many areas large-scale cash or credit dealing in food appears to have been limited to the early summer months.

Faced with the scarcities of the famine years, food prices rocketed. Figures on food prices during the famine years are difficult to disentangle with any precision. Most available statistics deal with wholesale prices, generally in central markets such as Dublin. These fluctuated less dramatically than retail prices in more remote areas, while sources suggest that much higher prices were charged for small than for large quantities by local hucksters. Nevertheless, Barrington's price index gives some indication of the changes which took place, but it is worth noting that his figures are the arithmetical mean of prices for the year and so understate the increases by a considerable amount.

IRISH AGRICULTURAL PRICES DURING THE FAMINE YEARS

(1840 equals 100)

	1845	1846	1847	1848	1849
Wheat	98	131	98	87	66
Oats	118	187	107	196	83
Barley	118	175	116	100	85
Potatoes	88	323	254	292	215
Butter	92	105	99	87	74
Pork	92	117	149	115	88
Mutton	120	120	125	120	105
Beef	103	104	105	110	79

On the Fassaroe estate in Co. Wicklow, potatoes which had been 4/4 (21p) per barrel in 1844 averaged 17/8 (88p) in 1846, a four-fold increase, and are estimated to have touched 30/- (£1.50) at peak price.[20]

Not surprisingly potatoes showed the largest price increase during the famine years, but oats and barley were obviously close dietary substitutes and their prices showed a sharp increase both in 1846 and in the later famine year of 1848. Wheat prices were much less affected, indicating that wheat did not form part of the normal Irish peasant diet, being too expensive. This is even more the case with respect to beef, mutton and butter prices which appear to have been almost impervious to the famine. Pork prices rose, partly reflecting their role in the peasant diet, but more likely because the cost of keeping a pig rose sharply with the shortage of potatoes.

Potatoes had been favoured by the Irish labouring class partly because they apparently liked them, but also because they were the cheapest staple foodstuff normally available. With the unprecedented rise in potato prices and scarcity of supply, the labouring population was forced to substitute alternative foods such as oats or Indian meal. Indigenous supplies of oats were grossly inadequate to meet the shortfall and Indian meal, the cheapest grain available on international markets, became the substitute staple during the famine years, and indeed for at least a generation thereafter. Contrary to popular opinion, Indian meal was not unknown in Ireland before the famine; there are records of it being imported into Ulster during the scarce season of 1800-2 when it apparently cost less than half the price of an equivalent quantity of oatmeal. It was also used during the scarce year of 1827 when Callan schoolteacher, Humphrey O'Sullivan, records its distribution, noting, 'Many people like it well: it will keep down the cost of living for the poor'. Pre-famine imports, however, remained small, further confirming the theory that during those years Ireland probably contained adequate supplies of food. Margaret Crawford estimates total imports between 1804 and 1844 at 29,432 cwts. compared with 5,833,014 cwts. during the famine years 1845-49.[21] Even this considerable importation was inadequate, particularly during the winter of 1846 and the early months of 1847, when even Indian meal prices showed a sharp increase. Prices in the early months of 1846 appear to have averaged 1d per lb., or marginally higher; by the late autumn and winter of that year prices in excess of 2d were the norm, and peaks of 2.4 and 2.88d were recorded during January 1847 after which time prices began to drop sharply.[22] Wicklow landlord's wife, Elizabeth Smith records in her diary for 26th September 1846, '2/8 (13½p.) for a stone of meal, I have known it at a shilling (5p.)'.[23]

Unfortunately it is not possible to accurately relate the price of subsisting on Indian meal to the cost of surviving on potatoes in prefamine years, but a doubling in the cost of a basic subsistence diet during 1846 could be taken as conservative; a trebling in subsistence costs in the period December 1846–January 1847 is not improbable.

To the initial problem of supply one could add the dependence of the peasantry on local shopkeepers who were not averse to creaming off a substantial profit. Prices were highest for sales of small quantities. In Roscommon, in December 1846, meal cost 2/9 (14p.) per stone if bought in a one stone bag, or 3/4 (16p.) per stone if sold in pounds.[24] Some element of price competition, plus easier transport facilities, moderated price levels in the larger towns and cities; prices were considerably higher in the more remote areas. It was estimated that prices in Lettermore, Connemara, were more than 25% higher than prices in Galway, a journey of twenty-six miles.[25] The absence of an established retail food market in the more isolated rural areas forced people to walk long distances, ten, twenty or even thirty miles to buy food according to one source, though small food traders invariably mushroomed, selling at prices often 30% above the already-high market price.[26] The dependence on shopkeepers' credit also increased real prices. Many workers found their earnings already fully committed in advance to repay the cost of credit dealings. However, with the persistence of famine conditions credit became more difficult to obtain.

It is the rise in prices which resulted from the scarcity of food, rather than mere food scarcity per se which is central to the Irish famine. Famines are caused, as the Indian economist Sen has pointed out, not by a shortage of food, but by a loss of entitlement to food. While the initial problem in Ireland was the failure of the potato crop, famine and excess deaths would not have occurred if the Irish peasantry had been able to command alternative food supplies at a price within their means. The evidence of the *Poor Inquiry* reveals that, in normal circumstances, the labouring and cottier classes had few surplus resources and most were forced to either get food on credit or to beg for some during the hungry months of the early summer. During the famine the rapid escalation of food prices put adequate nutrition out of the reach of labourers' pockets. On 24 February 1846 Elizabeth Smith's diary noted: 'Potatoes now 5d a stone. Jemmy Craig's — a labourer on a nearby farm whose total cash income was 2/- (10p.) plus *his* food. When rent 6d (2½p.) and tobacco 3d (1½p.) was paid there remained 1/3 (6p.) to buy food and clothing for his wife and three children — wife cannot do with less than ten stone in the week so 50d (21p.) per week on an income of 15d (6p.)'.[27] The following week when prices had risen even higher she noted that 'potatoes at their present price would take 9/- (45p.) a week. Labourers can earn a *maximum* 6/- (30p.)'. Food prices rose to considerably higher levels during the winter of 1846-7 and by the end of November she recorded that 'At present prices it would require 21/- (£1.05) a week to support a labourer and his family; he earns 6/- (30p.), 7/- (35p.) or 8/- (40p.) at the highest. What must be the result?'[28] This problem was universal among the labouring and small farming class. Board of Works official, Mr. Lowe, wrote from Timoleague in West Cork in January 1847 that

Indian meal and wheaten meal are both selling at 2/6 (12½p.) for 14 lbs. — a family of five persons cannot on wages of 6/- (30p.) per week have even two meals for four days in the week.[29]. . .

The purchase of food became the sole priority for the Irish poor and to do so they liquidated all available assets, borrowed where possible and economised on all other items. William Forster, who was investigating conditions in the west of Ireland on behalf of the Society of Friends, noted in Connemara:

> When there before I had seen cows at almost every cabin and there were besides many sheep and pigs owned in the village. But now all the sheep were gone; all the cows, all the poultry killed; not one pig left; the very dogs which had barked at me before had disappeared; no potatoes, no oats, workmen unpaid; patient, quiet look of despair.[30]. . .

A report to the Society of Friends from Dunfanaghy, Co. Donegal noted that

> The small farmers and cottiers had parted with all their pigs and their fowl, and even their bed-clothes and fishing-nets had gone for one object; the supply of food.[31]

A correspondent wrote from Arklow in February 1847

> So long as the poor, that is the general class of inhabitants, had any articles whether of clothing, furniture, fish or agricultural implements to pawn the extent of distress remained unknown; but now that all is gone. . . .[32]

while a Mr. Prendergast, an inspector of drainage for the Board of Works, writing from Carrigallen, Ballinamore, Co. Leitrim stated emphatically in February 1847

> Famine actually prevails and deaths are frightfully numerous from want and disease caused by insufficient food and clothing. Some poor women were in the town before daylight last market day to conceal their bedding and few articles of furniture. They were *to be sold for a few days' food.* A man in the town, himself half stupefied by want and wandering in and out of doorways without asking for aid. A woman lately mentioned the excellent soup she had made *after killing her cow*, there being no other resource. Now that speaks volumes, for the pigs being already gone and the poultry too, there will remain absolutely nothing but the meal in the market for all provisions.[33]

The impact of rocketing food prices spread widely. Fishermen, despite the undoubted food scarcity, found themselves without customers. Fish was regarded as a luxury; all available resources were committed to buying potatoes, meal or bread[34] and Claddagh fishermen were forced to pawn their fishing equipment to survive.[35] Pawnbrokers also found themselves in difficulty. There were plenty of clients wishing to pledge items, but no buyers, and they found their capital locked up in unsaleable items.[36]

While cottiers and labourers were the most immediate victims of the famine because of their greater dependence on potatoes as food and the lack of resources which they could sell to command food, small farmers were also severely affected. Many were forced to eat their grain as a substitute for diseased potatoes, or they had to sell farm animals, partly because with the loss of potatoes there was no food for pigs, because the high price of oats made feeding a horse prohibitively expensive or simply because they needed the money to buy food. Many who were not threatened with actual starvation suffered a sharp drop in their living standards as a result of the exceptional rise in the price of food and no longer had money to spend on other items. As the Central Relief Committee noted

> Prices were so high that those who were still able to maintain themselves and their families could not afford to spend any money except on food. The small shopkeepers consequently lost their trade. The business of the wholesale dealer and merchant was diminished. The various branches of manufactures felt the want of demand; many of the work-people were discharged. Few houses were repaired or built, and masons, carpenters and other tradesmen connected with building were left unemployed. The demand for clothes, notwithstanding the great want of them, which was everywhere felt, decreased. Tailors, shoemakers and other tradesmen of this class accordingly suffered. The gentry whose rents were not paid, and who had poor-rates added to their other incumbrances, reduced their spending.[37]

Not everyone lost as a result of the famine. Those with sufficient cash and acumen to buy grain in advance of maximum demand undoubtedly gained, as did larger farmers who found the increased cost of their food more than counterbalanced by the high prices which they earned from selling their surplus grain. Their diet would have been less dependent on potatoes than that of the small farmers and labourers, so that their cost of living would have risen by less than average, though heavier poor rates could take their toll. Small farmers generally lost out, first because in many cases they were net consumers rather than net producers of grain, but also because, even when they had surplus grain, they were forced to sell it early in the season, often uncut, because of financial difficulties and so could not reap the maximum financial benefit. In February 1847 Elizabeth Smith noted

> Provisions are rising every market. Thus the large farmer is doing well, his produce selling for three times the price of an ordinary year, his consumption though more costly, still very fairly proportional to his profit. The small farmer is ruined, he must let his corn, sell his stock at the unseasonable time because he has not fodder and therefore leave himself penniless for the coming year.[38]

One Cork poor law guardian noted in January 1847 that even respectable farmers of thirty acres were 'suffering severely at present as they are obliged to consume in their families and in their stables the corn which in former years procured clothing and other comforts for them'.[39]

Farmer-Labourer relations

The failure of the potato crop totally undermined the economic basis of rural Ireland and destroyed traditional relationships. Bound labourers or cottiers worked for farmers, not for direct cash payments, but to offset the cost of potato ground which they rented from the farmer; unbound labourers worked for cash but rented potato ground independently which they paid for either from wage earnings, or perhaps from the sale of part of their conacre crop. With the failure of potatoes a conacre plot became worthless since it could no longer guarantee food for the coming year. Labourers therefore saw little value in continuing to work for a farmer to pay the rent of a now-useless plot of land; many demanded payment in cash which alone would provide them with food, and, when farmers generally refused, they deserted to search for cash employment on other farms, in the towns and increasingly on public works. In Co. Cork this form of labourer militancy emerged in the autumn of 1845 with the first partial potato failure; in retaliation many farmers refused to rent conacre for the 1846 season unless labourers paid some or all of their rent in advance, a demand that few could meet. In consequence the Co. Cork conacre acreage fell by 20% in 1846.[40]

The 1846 failure compounded this disruption as labourers deserted their plots and farm work en masse in search of ready cash and higher earnings elsewhere. With the sharp increase in the price of subsistence foodstuffs, the minimum cost of labour—the cost of feeding workers—rose. Farmers with live-in farm servants whom they fed or those who were paid a lower wage but provided with food, found the cost of feeding labour a major burden. One Board of Works official based in Co. Cavan reported that 'the high price of food not only of itself aggravates it (distress) but compels farmers, who formerly used to give 4d a day and food, to discharge their labour'.[41] Labourers who were not dieted were forced to campaign for higher wages in order to survive at a time when many farmers were themselves under financial pressure because of the potato failure. The pressure on farmers to increase money wages was compounded by the availability of jobs on public works schemes, jobs paying regular wages often at levels farmers could not afford. Complaints of a scarcity of labourers on farms were rife by the spring of 1847. The lower acreage of potatoes planted in 1847 reflected not only a shortage of seed, but also the disruption of old farming practices, notably the extensive use of labour which was paid in conacre ground. Complaints of a shortage of labour and the reduced crop acreage in 1847 tend to disprove the common assertion that pre-famine Ireland was overrun with unemployed workers made, for example, by Trevelyan in *The Irish crisis*

> a fortnight planting, a week or ten days digging and fourteen days turf cutting suffice for his subsistence. During the rest of the year he is at leisure to follow his own inclinations.[42]

The increased price of labour brought an end to many of the old labour-intensive practices, notably the careful manuring of potato ground with seaweed, sand and animal manure.[43] Larger farmers economised on labour as best they could. Hired labour was dispensed with. By the winter of 1846 several officers in charge of relief works reported an influx of labourers 'that have been during some time past, in constant employment of the farmers, not so much perhaps of their own pleasure as on account of the farmers refusing them further assistance'.[44] In the absence of hired labour, the volume of tillage farming fell. Many accounts of rural Ireland by the autumn of 1846, and increasingly in the spring of 1847, note the absence of tillage work in progress. In October 1846, Lt. Col. Jones wrote from Newry

> The weather has been favourable; and the ground in a good state and not a single plough have I seen at work or any land being turned up by hand labour; all the land of the country appears to be laying fallow. The fields have the appearance of being deserted.[45]

In many instances farmers substituted family for hired labour. One account from Co. Waterford early in 1847 noted

> A plough is now occasionally seen on the farms but instead of labourers being employed the farmers' sons guide the plough. The farmers can scarcely be blamed for dismissing new servants, having so little food for themselves in very many instances.[46]

The Changing Structure of Agriculture During the Famine Years

It was no longer possible to sustain pre-famine farming practices and in response to both the higher cost of labour and, no doubt, fears of falling grain prices in the aftermath of the repeal of the corn laws, there was a significant shift from tillage to pasture, particularly on large farms. Cattle numbers rose from 1,840,025 (excluding calves) in 1841 to 2,591,415 (including calves) in 1847 and further increased to 2,917,949 by 1850 — a process which continued in subsequent years. However cattle numbers fell on smaller holdings, rising sharply on those over thirty acres.

CHANGING CATTLE NUMBERS BY SIZE OF FARM[47]

	1847	1850	% change
Farms under 1 ac.	39,742	27,093	−31.8%
1-5	83,389	68,168	−18.3%
5-15	391,155	398,458	+1.86%
15-30	545,772	583,152	+6.85%
30 plus	1,482,951	1,847,315	+24.6%
Total	2,591,415	2,917,949	+12.6%

Some of the decline on the smaller holdings, and the corresponding increase on the larger reflects a shift in average size of farm, but this only confirms the general picture of a shift from more labour-intensive tillage farming, as practiced on smaller holdings, to more capital-intensive grazing.

The change was not only attributable to the departure of labourers from the larger farms. Small farmers who generally survived on a potato diet and sold grain for cash to pay their rents were forced during famine years to consume the grain themselves, and, with nothing left to pay their rent, tended to neglect their farms in the belief that eviction was inevitable in the near future.[48] Faced with the need to devote more of their farm output to feeding their families, many small farmers no longer felt that their holdings were viable at existing rents. One public works official wrote in the spring of 1847

> There are no signs of a desire on the part of the holders of ten acres and under to cultivate their land. They say that rents are too high and as they could barely afford to pay them in good seasons with potatoes they will be utterly incapable of

doing so if their land is sown with grain. They therefore consider it better to earn something on the roads (which all goes into their pockets) than to incur the expense and liabilities for the benefit of others.[49]

Financial hardship also left such men without capital; they were forced to sell off livestock, or were already so in debt that they were unable to borrow funds for seed and other agricultural necessities. The decline in the number of small farms is therefore not surprising, even ignoring the active role of the landlord in evicting farmers, which we will examine later.

CHANGING SIZE AND NUMBER OF FARMS 1845-51[50]

	1845	1851
1-5 acres	181,950	88,083
5-15 acres	311,133	191,854
15 plus	276,618	290,401
Total	769,701	570,338

The Government's Response

As previously indicated, this was not the first time that Ireland had sought assistance in time of threatened famine. Since 1816-17 there had been regular injections of state assistance, primarily in the west of Ireland, to meet seasons of scarcity. In addition, British charitable agencies had made generous contributions. By 1845 the Irish problem was being seen as a chronic social problem to be resolved by a major restructuring both of Irish agriculture and of rural society: a restructuring designed to contain the seemingly endless population increase and bring Irish society into the nineteenth century. Trevelyan, the assistant secretary to the treasury, and one of the key figures in famine relief administration wrote in his book *The Irish crisis*

> The relations of employer and employee which form together the framework of society, and establish a mutual dependence and good-will, have no existence in the potato system. The Irish small-holder lives in a state of isolation — the type of which is to be sought for in the islands of the South Sea, rather than in the great civilised communities of the ancient world.[51]

The Anglo-Irish landlords were seen as primarily responsible for perpetuating this 'primitive' system by tolerating rampant subdivision and rapid population growth on their estates. Elizabeth Smith, the Scottish-born wife of a modest Wicklow landlord, wrote in her diary

> The Irish landlord is in no essential different from the Irish peasant — his superior position has raised him in many points above his labouring countryman but the character of this race is common to all. The same carelessness or recklessness, call it what you will — the same indolence, the same love of pleasure, the same undue appreciation of self. The landlords that are not popular are what we should call the good ones who look after their affairs.[52]

Irish famine was therefore increasingly seen not as an act of God, but as the nemesis for landlord indifference and neglect. Trevelyan wrote that the Irish landlords alone 'had it in their power to restore society to a safe and healthy state'.[53] With such views in common currency the prospect of London footing the entire bill for Irish famine relief was remote: it would be placed as far as possible on the shoulders of those who were responsible for the disasters — the Irish landlords. Thomas Drummond's ringing injunction to the Tipperary landlords, 'property has its duties as well as its rights', had a considerable financial sting in its tail.

By the mid 1840s Ireland faced the problem that its appeal for famine relief was no longer a novelty, while the dramatic impact of harrowing accounts of Irish poverty was beginning to wear thin. There were some allegations — how true it is difficult to say — that accounts of distress in the west of Ireland had been magnified in order to maximise relief. Power le Poer Trench, Church of Ireland archbishop of Tuam, who was heavily involved in relief operations in the west wrote

> Starvation is now become a trade, and provisions are sent in abundance where no calamity occurred and where there is no extraordinary need to warrant it. The cry is, as the provision is going, why should not that parish get its share. . . . Places that I know were never in less want than they are this year have received large supplies of meal.[54]

By the time of the famine in the 1840s the British government had also come to distrust alarmist reports of famine in Ireland. Sir Robert Peel apparently believed that all reports from the executive in Ireland needed careful scrutiny because 'a haze of exaggeration covered Dublin Castle like a fog'.[55]

In rural Ireland, concerned individuals, particularly landlords who had been actively involved in famine relief and fund raising in the past, were less forthcoming. Many felt that they were making an adequate contribution to the poor via the rates paid to finance the new workhouses and scaled down their charity accordingly. Elizabeth Smith, as early as 1841, noted increasing difficulty in raising funds at her local church for the protestant poor of the area, because people argued that they were already saddled with some of the burden of relieving the poor, who had been neglected by their absentee or less socially-responsible neighbours.[56] Sir Randolph Routh, who carried major responsibility for Irish famine relief, told Trevelyan in 1846 that 'a great many landed proprietors had refused altògether' to subscribe to famine relief schemes.[57]

Increased sectarianism and allegations of souperism also disrupted local relief efforts, though many protestant clergymen were actively involved in famine relief during those years. Almost all the grants given by the Society of Friends were locally administered by Church of Ireland clergy. Many of these clergy and their wives manned soup boilers, while catholic priests were constantly engaged in administering the last rites to dying people.[58] Evidence of Church of Ireland involvement is best indicated by the fact that, in the year 1847, forty protestant clergy died from famine fever, while the famine also claimed the lives of many catholic clergy. Some relief work was carried out by joint co-operation between catholic and protestant clergy, but divisions were all too common both between clergy of different religions and between influential local laymen. Applications for famine relief from individuals, rather than committees, were common, and Bowen noted that, during the famine years, 'Catholic Protestant suspicions often led to the breakdown of this tradition of self-governing aristocratic method of government'.[59] This breakdown lessened the efficiency of local relief efforts and in the process probably cost lives.

This lack of social cohesion coupled with the British belief that Ireland and Irish landlordism were in need of a severe shock undoubtedly served to weaken the effectiveness of response to the great famine. Some saw the crisis and suffering as almost inevitable. Thus Elizabeth Smith, when food prices reached their peak in January 1847 wrote

> I don't know what will become of us before spring. We have no right to look to rich England for help, no right to expect the government to take charge of our private affairs. We have brought our miseries upon ourselves; a long series of improvident management results in ruin.[60]. . .

The existence of such beliefs among Irish landlords coupled with the strong social and political divisions prevailing in the country, plus O'Connell's personal antipathy towards Sir Robert Peel, meant that there was no strong political demand made from Ireland, even by a section of the Irish political leadership, for Irish famine relief to become a United Kingdom charge. Such a possibility was further reduced by the fact that the Scottish highlands were also threatened by famine, while the mid 1840s were a time of undoubted social distress in industrial England.[61] For some of those involved, such as Trevelyan, the famine was retrospectively viewed as a providential suffering designed to reform Irish society. In words reminiscent of a Calvinist preacher he wrote that 'on this as on many other occasions, the Supreme Wisdom had educed permanent good out of transient evil'.[62] Against this complex social and political background, and given the magnitude of the economic and social upheaval which resulted from the potato failure, the question of government famine relief becomes immensely complicated.

Government Famine Relief Policy
Food Depots

Sir Robert Peel, the British prime minister when potato blight first appeared in 1845, was undoubtedly the British politician with the greatest experience of Irish social problems. As a young chief secretary for Ireland in 1817 he had initiated the relief measures of that year.[63] According to his biographer, Norman Gash, already by October 1845 Peel had 'virtually made up his mind that he was facing a major disaster in Ireland'.[64] His response to the Irish famine, however, became inextricably bound up with the repeal of the corn laws, which had restricted the free importation of grain into the United Kingdom. Peel had already decided that the corn laws, the last barrier towards complete free trade, must be removed.[65] The Irish famine merely provided the justification for that step and in practice was 'little more than a side issue' in the major political debate over free trade in food.[66] Its greatest consequence may have been the split in the British conservative party which resulted in the fall of Peel's government in June 1846 and its replacement by a Whig government led by Lord John Russell.[67]

Peel's response to the potato failure has generally been favourably regarded in Ireland — a matter of some interest given the strong hostility which most of his measures aroused. The phrase from the generally-hostile *Freeman's Journal* that 'no man died of famine during his administration'[68] is frequently quoted. He has been praised for showing 'an initiative unusual in that era of laissez faire and (because) he undertook tasks at variance with current economic theory'.[69] Perhaps his personal experiences of being in Ireland during the earlier shortage of 1817 gave him a degree of emotional involvement which the following outburst would seem to indicate.

> Good God, are you to sit in cabinet, and consider and calculate how much diarrhoea, and bloody flux, and dysentery, a people can bear before it becomes necessary for you to provide them with food.[70]. . .

On the other hand, Peel was only dealing with a partial food failure: there was probably enough food in the country in 1845-6 to feed everybody and small farmers still held assets in the form of savings and livestock. The dizzy rise in food prices did not begin until the autumn of 1846, after Peel had left office, though the food price stability may be partly due to the operation of his government food depots. Indian meal prices remained virtually stable at 1-1.2d per lb. until the autumn of 1846; wheat prices averaged 47/- per cwt. on the market in August 1846 but reached 70/- by January 1847 and 100/- by the following May.[71]

Peel's relief measures in 1845-6 were not remarkably dissimilar to those which he had introduced in 1817, or from those which had been used, with apparent efficacy, during the intervening years. A relief commission representing army, police and coastguard services, the poor law commission and Dublin Castle administration, with distinguished scientist Sir Robert Kane as token catholic, was established to organise food depots and stimulate the formation of local committees which would organise relief works.

The establishment of food depots and the secret purchase of stocks of Indian meal on the international market through the London bankers Baring Bros. are the items of Peel's relief policy which have generally attracted most praise, particularly when contrasted with the more dogmatic approach to the role of government adopted by the subsequent Whig administration. In November 1845 Peel and Goulburn, his chancellor of the exchequer, ordered that £100,000 be spent on buying Indian corn for secret shipment and storage in Ireland and this decision was implemented even before treasury sanction had been obtained.[72]

Ultimately over £185,000 was spent on the food scheme, over £105,000 on purchasing food in the U.S., almost £46,000 on buying stocks of Indian meal and oatmeal in Britain and £6,544 on buying oatmeal in Ireland. The remainder went on freight and grinding corn.[73] Of the total, £135,000 was recovered from sales. Food was sold through government depots, either in small quantities to private customers or to local relief committees for resale. Police and coastguards operated sub-depots in areas which lacked local committees, notably in the west of Ireland.[74] The supply of food from government depots, generally sold at cost price as a mixture of Indian meal and some oatmeal, was designed not to provide for the whole market, but to act as a brake on the tendency of local traders to increase prices unduly. Total stocks represented only two week's food for one million people, while the fact that depots did not open until the late spring of 1846, the first on 28 March, some not until June,[75] indicates that the pressure on food supplies was not unduly severe.

In fact private enterprise was not unsuccessful at responding to the Irish food shortage during the 1845-46 season. Indian meal imports, a mere trickle in previous years, rose very sharply during 1845 and early 1846; of these Peel's much publicised contribution, none of which arrived before February 1846, amounted to a 'mere trickle', at most perhaps ten per cent. One author has stated that 'the extent of government interference with the grain trade was trifling in comparison with the overall figures'.[76] In addition, local relief committees also organised food depots, devoting a considerable proportion of the £112,000 which they raised in subscriptions and £104,000 provided in government loans to that purpose.[77]

Peel's government fell in the summer of 1846. Faced with a total potato failure the Whig government did not continue his policy of direct government importation of food, perhaps because of a greater ideological commitment to laissez-faire economics and partly because circumstances in the autumn of 1846 were considerably more difficult. In 1845-6 Peel's policy of purchasing food may have been successful (it is in fact difficult to estimate its precise contribution) but by 1846 the government had lost the element of surprise and secrecy. The government depots angered small traders as one official described

> A feeling of jealous anger was aroused at first among the small dealers against the government, men who living as wretchedly to all appearances as the rest of the community nevertheless possess some money to lay it out in meals or potatoes.[78]

Private traders apparently threatened not to import food into Ireland unless the government gave an assurance, duly given in the early autumn of 1846, that it would not continue its food imports.[79] In fact the government food depots were retained in the west of Ireland, and contrary to its promise the government did import some food to provision these depots.

Obtaining sufficient food for the limited number of depots proved difficult. The autumn and winter of 1846-7 was a time of considerable scarcity throughout Europe. High prices on the continent caused grain shipments from the Black Sea to be landed in France or Belgium rather than England, while with a buoyant food trade shipping costs for grain from either the U.S.A. or the Black Sea rose sharply.[80] Britain was also affected by food scarcity and by a major industrial depression which lasted until 1849.

In October 1846 Trevelyan wrote of his determination

> *without being in the least deterred by considerations of expense* to establish as many meal stations in the west of Ireland as we can hope to keep regularly supplied; but there is another consideration which must put a general limit to our operations in this respect, which is, that *this* year there is a general scarcity over the whole of the U.K. . . . to buy up without restraint supplies intended for the English and Scotch markets would merely have the effect of transferring the famine from one country where the people are fed out of the public purse to one where they are struggling to maintain themselves; and it would not be tolerated that the English and Scotch labourers should not only have to support the Irish labourers (for it is always the mass of the population which pays the bulk of the taxes) but that the price of necessaries of life should also be raised upon the former to a famine price by an unrestrained consumption of those in Ireland.[81]

In fact the government only managed to import a total of 4,800 tons for its stores in the west and resisted pressure in later months to extend food depots into eastern counties on the grounds that they had failed to gain sufficient supplies even to fill the existing depots.[82]

There were therefore genuine practical difficulties to repeating Peel's food policy and it remains questionable whether activity on his scale could have had any significant effect in the much more critical conditions of 1846-7. Peel's depots had not opened before the end of March, by October 1846 an engineer in charge of public works in Borris in Ossory (not the most destitute part of the country) wrote

> Unless actually seen, it is difficult to form a correct conception of the wretched state in which the labourers and many of the poor farmers now are. It is not a very unusual thing for men who have been only a few days on our works to work all day without eating one morsel but during the hours for breakfast and dinner, lie down behind a fence, unwilling to be seen by those who have something to eat.[83]

Many saw government non-interference in the food market as desirable to produce the maximum level of supplies. The new Irish chief secretary, Henry Labouchere, wrote to Daniel O'Connell that 'the great object at this moment appears to me to be to protect the trade in food'.[84]

Precisely how much food was in the country was a matter of debate. Several accounts from officials involved with relief works in the autumn of 1846 speak of haggards and barns full of unthreshed grain. According to British prime minister, Lord John Russell, farmers, who the previous year had sold their corn early at comparatively low prices and then seen prices rise sharply, were reluctant to repeat the experience.[85] It was felt that non-interference in the market, letting food prices rise, would attract the sale of available produce and encourage imports. The endorsement of the primacy of the unrestricted food market was not limited to the Whig government. Fr. Theobold Mathew, the temperance friar, in the course of a letter complaining about the number of public houses which had opened up in the vicinity of relief works wrote

> I feel pleasure in stating that the non-interference of the Government in the purchase of corn, though productive of much suffering has eventuated in an abundant supply of grain. Prices are rapidly declining; and I confidently hope that our population will enjoy a comfortable and comparatively happy Christmas.[86]

The good friar was a poor predictor of price trends; prices soared in midwinter, peaking towards the end of January. The Society of Friends, whose charitable endeavours have occasioned much praise in most accounts of the famine, was equally committed to protecting the private food market, even in the west of Ireland. They considered the possibility of sending food to the west but

> After considerable discussion it was decided that it was not desirable to make shipments of any of those articles in which merchants usually dealt. We felt the propriety of leaving the supply of the market to private traders.[87]

Instead of meal they supplied rice to starving western peasants, confident that they were not directly competing with the food trade of local hucksters.

Public Works

Given the various problems, real or imaginary, associated with food distribution, the main burden of famine relief rested with the tried and trusted remedy of public works, a remedy which had been used on an almost regular basis in the previous thirty years. In 1846, as in previous seasons, the administrative burden for supervising public works fell primarily on the Board of Works. The British cabinet decided that public works should be jointly financed, with half the cost coming from local taxation, the balance in the form of a treasury grant. Legislation allowing for this was passed in March 1846, while Peel also introduced measures to encourage land drainage and the construction of piers for the fishing industry.[88] Applications for government finance were forwarded by the local grand juries, (the bodies responsible for levying rates); the Board of Works then examined the proposed schemes and approved or rejected the loans. Employment was given to those with relief tickets from local relief committees— bodies generally consisting of active local landlords, or their representatives, local clergy and any others who had made donations to famine relief schemes. In the late spring of 1846 road works and river drainage schemes commenced throughout most Irish counties. Ultimately a maximum of 97,617 were employed and, by August 1846, works were in progress in every county except Derry, Tyrone, Fermanagh, Armagh and Down. In addition some of the local committees operated their own relief works. By August 1846 there had been claims for works costing £1,292,853-8-7 of which £458,143-13-6 was sanctioned.[89]

Public works were deemed necessary to provide the labouring population with sufficient money to buy food. Officials realised that measures to increase food supplies alone would not prove sufficient. Dobree, the deputy commissary, wrote in March 1846

> Although the large rations of food on private account must increase the means of supply in the country I scarcely see how they will operate in relieving the distress unless wages available for labour are within the paupers' reach.[90]

Awareness that government money was available for relief works led to the inevitable rash of applications. The barony of Moyarta in Clare submitted a total of 96 road schemes, neighbouring Inchiquin 113.[91] Galway commissioners demanded money for sewerage, or for a new barracks; Limerick wanted money for a railway line. In the autumn of 1846 when relief works were resumed after summer suspension, virtually every obscure prospective Irish railway company wrote in search of government funds.[92] Col. Jones, public works commissioner, was highly critical of the whole process.

> It appears to be a system for each barony to apply for as much money as they think the Government will grant . . . memorials are not sent in until the demands for work become pressing. . .

while they had received demands from areas 'when that same day's post has brought up reports from an officer in the same district that there is no immediate necessity for work'.[93] Charges of excessive dependence on the government were common. Thus Mr. Dobree wrote to Trevelyan from Waterford

> From all that I can collect no measures whatever have been adopted in any part of this district (beyond private charities) to afford relief when the crisis may come. It appears evident that those persons on whom the moral responsibility is constitutionally vested are doing nothing more than thinking upon what the Government is going to do, intending thereby to oblige Government to take the initiative and to throw the onus upon their shoulder.[94]

Sir Randolph Routh, the commissary general, wrote to Trevelyan that his impression from various relief committee meetings was that people tended to 'apply to the Government first and then to subscribe afterwards'.[95] Several areas failed to establish relief committees; in other cases committees divided into factions—there were disputes among a relief committee in Kilkee, Co. Clare as early as January 1846. In 1845-46 there is some impression of government officials attempting to remedy shortcomings in the local committee system, establishing food depots and endeavouring to shore up inadequacies. There is little doubt, however, that relief works were established, not simply on the basis of need, but in response to active local lobbyists. Reviewing the position in July 1846, Jones noted

> There is no doubt that many works were commenced without necessity. It is true that the representations were extremely urgent and pressing and very great precautions and judgement were necessary.[96]

Officials were faced with trying to distinguish between exceptional need due to potato failure and the normal distress which characterised Irish rural society.

An examination of the breakdown of expenditure on relief works in the period up to August 1846 suggests some relationship between allocation and above-average potato failure. Co. Clare, for example, received much the largest amount of public works money, over £75,000, followed by Co. Galway with almost £64,000. The generally prosperous county of Antrim received £14,000—mostly at the beginning of relief operations, no doubt reflecting heavy potato failure, but other apparently badly affected counties such as Monaghan or Waterford received very small sums indeed, Monaghan a mere £1,100. Co. Roscommon which appears to have been relatively severely affected received only about 40% of the sum granted to Co. Clare when allowance is made for their respective populations.[97] However these imbalances in relief expenditure do not appear to have occasioned major grievances, nor is there evidence that areas poorly served by relief works suffered significantly more than other areas. The greatest indicator of the lack of real pressure in 1845-6 is the fact that relief works did not begin until the late spring; by 31 March only £70,325 worth of works had been approved,[98] yet there is no evidence of excess deaths in the first two-thirds of 1846.

The transition from Tory to Whig government in June 1846 did not bring any immediate change. A treasury minute of July 1846 ordered that relief works were to be brought to an end unless they were required 'for the relief of urgent distress', though schemes could be continued if the grand jury was prepared to bear the full cost of the extra works.[99] The desire to halt public works was motivated not purely by a desire to save money, or to preserve *laissez-faire* principles, but because of an awareness that by August the harvest had to be saved and that men who would normally do such work had been diverted to public works. One official wrote to the Board of Works that unless public works were suspended 'the harvest will not be finished cutting and, what is as bad, *enough turf will not be cut.*[100] However reports by early August that the potato crop had been totally destroyed by blight made another season of relief works almost inevitable.

The experience of 1845-6 had been somewhat misleading as a guide to the following year. Matters were dramatically different in the autumn and winter of 1846-47. The apparent success of the relief methods of the spring of 1846 appear to have engendered the belief that traditional famine relief measures would again prove sufficient to meet the Irish crisis. This was certainly the opinion of Board of Works commissioner Jones in May 1846.[101] The operations of spring 1846 had also given rise to some scepticism in both Board of Works and the treasury about the genuineness of Irish allegations of distress. Peel's legislation, which had provided grants from central funds equal to half the cost, was deemed to have encouraged excessive demands for public works. The new legislation passed in the autumn of 1846 provided that half the cost would be levied on grand juries, the balance to be provided by central funds, but in the form of a loan rather than a grant. All the cost was ultimately to be borne by local taxpayers. Local committees were regarded as having exercised undue authority over the choice of workers who were employed; their authority was now to be limited to drawing up lists of eligible workers with the final choice and responsibility for scrutinising the list lying with Board of

Works inspectors. The board itself was expanded from three to five members, a reflection of its increased powers.[102]

The majority of relief works were to consist of road works, as they had in previous years, while care was to be taken to ensure that public works would not convey undue benefit on any one individual. There was considerable pressure from Irish landlords to include drainage works within the provisions of the act. Board of Works commissioner Jones wrote of

> the drift of all the various suggestions made by the deputations—which is to obtain money for improving their estates, without their giving any personal undertaking for its repayment.[103]

In October it was provided that landlords could borrow from the relief fund for drainage purposes but they became responsible for the full repayment. Some drainage schemes were implemented, but they amounted to only 5% of the total cost of relief works.[104] The low proportion was a consequence, perhaps, of the bureaucracy involved, as O'Neill suggests, but also of the fact that landowners were reluctant to borrow money for private schemes when they knew that they would also be burdened with the cost of general relief works. Schemes which seemed attractive if the government or the general community paid the bill became less so when the landlord was made directly responsible.

Efforts to assist Irish railways through relief works were even less successful. The government was deluged by requests for financial assistance under the guise of famine relief from countless small railway companies. Government objections were raised on the grounds that English and Scottish railway companies would demand similar assistance, and that the measure would be more beneficial to railway shareholders than to distressed labourers; it was estimated that only one-third of the total cost would accrue to labourers, with most of the money being spent on materials.[105] However, the alteration which provided loans for private drainage schemes also covered railways, though only one company—the Waterford and Limerick railway company—took advantage of the provision.[106]

The administration of public works in the autumn and winter of 1846 posed insuperable difficulties. The potato crop had almost totally failed and the price of food rose sharply. Countless labourers and small farmers, knowing that no food remained, deserted the land in search of money wages. Pressure for relief works emerged at a considerably earlier date than in the previous season; the total number employed reached a peak of 750,000 in the spring of 1847. The administration of works on such a scale posed enormous problems which were compounded by the fact that works were widely scattered, many were in the most remote areas, and administrative staff were often new and inexperienced. Allegations of bureaucratic delays were common. On 14 December 1846 Rev. Jeremiah Sheahan, P.P. Clinlaurence, west Cork, wrote that on 18 September a presentment of £6,000 had been granted for employment of destitute workers, but that not one farthing had been spent.[107] Allegations of delays in getting money which had been sanctioned to remote areas were common;[108] government pay clerks were apparently reluctant to penetrate into remote areas such as Skibbereen.[109]

Faced with the clamour of distress much of the administrative machinery broke down. Lt. Col. Jones wrote rather despairingly to Routh, that 'what was possible and practicable with 50,000 men is no longer so with seven times that number'.[110] The most vital area was the allocation of employment. It was intended that local committees would draw up lists of those in need which would then be vetted by the Board of Works inspectors, but that system proved almost inoperable. The problems reflected the difficulties of depending on public works as the principal method of famine relief, combined with the greed, self-interest or desire for political authority of local individuals. One harrassed official wrote from Co. Monaghan

> it is now only too apparent that no assistance is to be expected from the farmers, and little if any from the landed proprietors; in fact in many instances, they are purposely throwing the labourers entirely on the public works; the clergy of all denominations are pressing for employment for their followers in the same way; in short I am beset morning, noon and night, by hundreds of them; and of late some impatience has shown itself. The Relief Committees have done little as yet but provide enormous lists of applicants for labour and are very dissatisfied when I object to them.[111]

Many landlords dispatched their tenantry to the public works in the hope that they would earn enough to pay their rents.[112] Others claimed that a landlord's tenants were given work places in proportion to the amount of taxation which he had paid.[113]

As a result of such interference many of those employed on public works were large farmers or their sons, while some of the most deserving were turned away. In Corofin, Co. Clare, the Board of Works inspector, Capt. Wynne, a man who was to suffer assault and an assassination attempt, discovered 'at least one hundred cases where the comfortable farmer has been left on the list, while his neighbour, possessed of nothing in the world but his spade and his limbs, has been struck off'. Similar experiences were reported from Clare Abbey and Kilmeady.[114] In fact representatives of more prosperous farming families were in a position to earn sums more than double that earned by ordinary labourers as they could rent horses, carts and other equipment to the works schemes.

In addition, many who were undoubtedly deserving of relief but utterly incapable of performing heavy work were also foisted on the relief works administrators, simply because in many areas no alternative form of relief was available, even for the aged and infirm, except in the workhouse. From an early point the British government had been afraid to grant outdoor relief (relief such as food to people in their own homes) even to the infirm because they feared that it would start an expenditure avalanche which could not be contained. Similarly charities such as the Society of Friends were worried about distributing free food lest it should pauperize the population.[115] The blind, lame and infirm had therefore no option but to join relief works — regardless of their physical capacity. This situation worsened as the winter progressed and the main breadwinner fell sick. Women and children took their places, forced on to the public works by the pressure of local committees or of individuals such as an active local priest. Lt. Downes who was in charge of works in Co. Waterford complained of his works 'being much retarded by women and children being placed on the works (by the Committees) with spades and shovels, who are quite unfit for such work'.[116] More sympathetically, one of those involved in relief work for the Society of Friends wrote

> it was melancholy in the extreme to see the women and girls labouring on the public roads. They were employed, not only in digging with the spade and with the pick, but in carrying loads of earth and turf on their backs and wheeling barrows like men, and breaking stones, while the poor neglected children were crouched, in groups, around the bits of lighted turf.[117]

Faced with such acute pressure from men demanding work the majority of public works overseers simply capitulated and admitted all, regardless of need, to employment. Returns of those on relief works in the autumn and winter of 1846-7 note the number of able-bodied men, infirm men, women and boys as a matter of course. The alternative would have been to refuse those who pressed for employment, as Captain Wynne did, but the result was 'to draw down upon himself and the Board all the odium and vindictive feelings of the poorer classes'.[118] Jones, the Board of Works commissioner, had suggested that it would be simpler to disband all local committees, but Trevelyan disagreed.[119]

The more acute problem which intensified as the winter came concerned wage rates. Trevelyan had attempted to insure in the spring of 1846 that wages paid on public works should be less than standard agricultural wages, but following disagreement among members of the cabinet and the Irish administration the proposal was dropped. His desire was motivated partly by a wish to save money, but also by a fear — which was more than justified — that there would be a heavy exodus of workers from farming to public works. Trevelyan lost his first attempt to control wages; in the autumn of 1846 with the prospect of an even greater influx to the public works the desire to reduce the attraction was even greater. Payment on this occasion was to be by task work and it was envisaged that average wages should be about 2d per day less than the normal wages prevailing in the district.[120] The introduction of piece work, which was apparently previously uncommon in Ireland, proved very unpopular. Many illiterate and inexperienced labourers could not understand the basis for the calculations, while a threatened reduction in standard public works wages in September 1846 brought near-riots in many areas. The response appears to have been to reduce the stringency of inspection. Most workers appear to have initially earned 8d or 10d per day without much effort, with task work in most cases providing a bonus, so that average earnings of approximately 1/- per day, were common, with some workers earning higher sums.[121]

Sharply escalating food prices, (the price of Indian meal approximately doubled between August and January) plus the onset of harsh winter weather — and the winter of 1846-7 was unusually severe — made the economics of survival virtually impossible. Wages which had been adequate to feed a family in August or September could no longer do so by November. One witness from Clare wrote on 6 November that 'the fact is incontestable that the rate of labourers' pay bears no reference whatever to the present price of provisions'. The standard wage of 10d (4p) a day was 'wholly inadequate with meal at 3/- (15p) a stone', which was 'not more than sufficient for an average family for one day'.[122] Food prices peaked in January, precisely the time when weather conditions were at their worst and men were frequently laid off or sent home early. Jones wrote that Captain Wynne in Clare had reported seeing 'women returning home from Ennis, crying with grief at their inability to purchase; the price being too high for the small sums their husbands or sons had earned upon the works'.[123] In turn high food prices reduced food available to relief workers, leaving them malnourished and increasingly incapable of heavy manual work. By January, Captain Wynne was writing from Clare that 'the people are starving notwithstanding the enormous extent of employment which it is scarcely possible to increase without producing disorder and confusion'.[124] Another inspector wrote of 'fine gangs of men who three weeks ago could earn 1/2 (6p.) a day, cannot now earn 6d (2½p.) a day at the same work and the same valuation'.[125]

One possible solution would have been higher wages but this would have simply increased the problems facing Irish farming which had already lost a high proportion of its able-bodied workforce in their search for cash wages on the relief works. Farmers and landlords were in most cases unable to match the wages paid on relief works — any increase in such wages would have compounded their difficulties. The Board of Works officials touring the country were fully aware of the neglect of agriculture and could foresee the long-term consequences in totally inadequate food supplies for the coming season. In an effort to provide some cash income for the needy, while ensuring that farming was not wholly neglected, they issued 'Circular 38' on 9 December, a proposal drafted by one of the commissioners, Sir Richard Griffith, that would provide simultaneous employment of labourers by both the Board of Works and local farmers on 'family task work'. Labourers, assisted by their families, were to be assigned the task of building a specified length of drain and it was envisaged that children would help by collecting the necessary stones. Any family who could complete sufficient work for a fortnight's pay in less than that time, e.g. 6 or 8 days, could devote the remaining days to its own farm work. Unfortunately the circular had been prepared without prior consultation with either the British government or the treasury. Whig prime minister, Lord John Russell, expressed himself 'much alarmed' by the proposal and emphasised that 'no Ministry could defend such a proceeding'. Trevelyan wrote immediately demanding its withdrawal.[126] The Board of Works officials — both in Dublin and in the field — had become increasingly sceptical of the efficacy of their relief programme. Captain Wynne wrote from Clare, 'I can take care that no lives be lost from want of employment; but I cannot undertake to prevent many deaths from want of food'.[127] By December Jones was writing to Trevelyan noting that 'neither the season of the year nor the state of the poor will permit of their being employed on outdoor work to entitle them to receive a donation' and urging that relief should be given to the aged and infirm in their own cabins by a local authority, and he continued to press this point.[128] By the end of February another Board of Works commissioner, William Mulvany, was writing to Trevelyan of the 'remarkable coincidence of statements' from Board of Works staff scattered throughout the country.

All emphasised that workers were becoming much weaker and increasingly incapable of performing public works tasks; that farming was totally neglected; supplies of seed were very scarce.[129] By this stage London had been persuaded of the failure of the public works policy—a conviction brought about by continual reports of conditions in Ireland, but probably even more so by the fact that deaths from starvation—some occurring among men employed on relief works— had been reported. In January 1847 Lord John Russell told the house of commons that the public works scheme was being abandoned and replaced by the hitherto dreaded system of outdoor relief.[130] Those who had previously worried about the dangers of massive pauperization were no longer concerned, perhaps because mass pauperization had already occurred.

The public works carried out in the autumn and winter of 1846-7 cost the enormous sum of £4,848,235, which it was initially intended would be recouped from the areas which had benefited from the expenditure. The sum amounted to £5.23 for every family in Ireland which the Census Commissioners in 1841 deemed to be dependent entirely on their own labour for subsistence, i.e. those without capital or other resources. As in the spring of 1846 there is no reason to assume that public expenditure was allocated to give the maximum benefit to those in greatest need. Evidence quoted above suggests problems with allocating work in many areas; perhaps of greater interest is the fact that public expenditure did not necessarily go to the areas of greatest need. Map 2 examines the allocation of expenditure on general relief works from August 1846, to January, 1847—the period of greatest emphasis on public works as a relief measure. The figures exclude expenditure on both land drainage schemes and fishery development, but this should not materially alter the picture as only 5% of total spending went on drainage while fishery expenditure was also insignificant.[131] While the map does indicate that in broad terms spending was higher towards the west of the country and lowest in north-east Ulster, it also indicates considerable discrepancies in spending patterns. As in the spring of 1846 Co. Clare again obtained a much greater sum for public works than any other area, though Co. Limerick was not far behind. While some parts of Galway and Mayo received relatively high sums, other undoubtedly deprived areas, such as Erris, or the Carbery baronies of West Cork, including the much publicised town of Skibbereen, received much lower amounts, lower in fact than a number of undoubtedly more prosperous areas in counties such as Kilkenny. In fact, examining figures on a county basis reveals that Co. Kilkenny spent a marginally greater sum per labouring

THE FAMINE

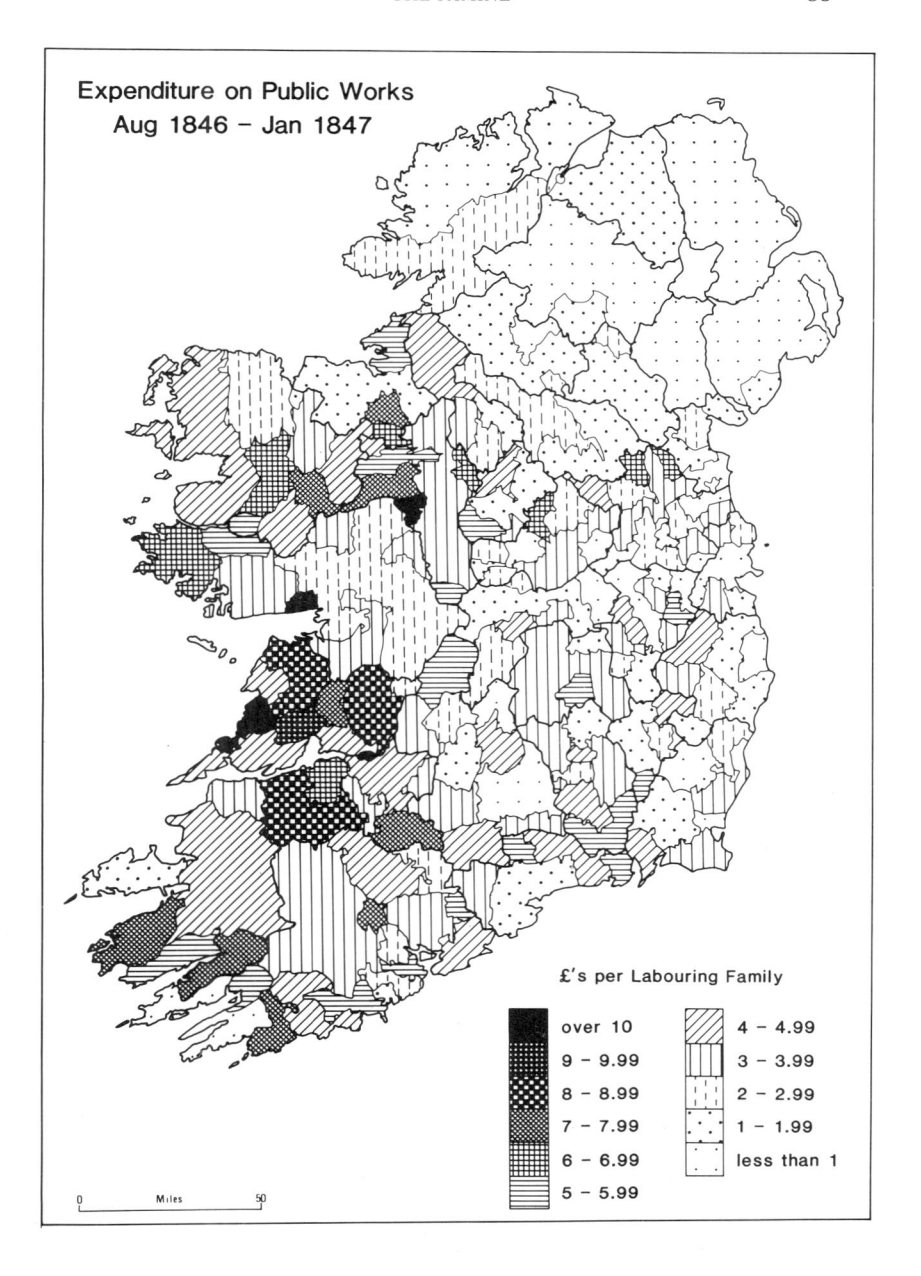

Expenditure on Public Works
Aug 1846 – Jan 1847

£'s per Labouring Family

- over 10
- 9 – 9.99
- 8 – 8.99
- 7 – 7.99
- 6 – 6.99
- 5 – 5.99
- 4 – 4.99
- 3 – 3.99
- 2 – 2.99
- 1 – 1.99
- less than 1

family than Co. Roscommon, and approximately one third more than Co. Galway. Prosperous Co. Kildare spent more than Co. Donegal and only marginally less than impoverished Leitrim. The imbalances in spending cannot be adequately explained. Property valuations in the most destitute areas were extremely low. Expenditure on famine relief works was determined by a combination of local lobbying, administrative acumen to propose works and apply for relief, plus belief in the financial ability to pay for it. Lack of active resident gentlemen in itself could account for a lack of applications to the Board of Works, as indeed could an active gentry class who were prepared to provide adequate employment from their own resources. Of the two the former may be the more accurate explanation. One Church of Ireland clergyman writing about conditions in the Skibbereen area, one of the regions whose famine conditions were most publicised, and an area where some of the first deaths from starvation were reported, wrote

> In none of the places where I was did the cases appear to be desperate; there is no want of food in any place — delightful consideration — nor want of medicine, but there is a most deplorable want of *available agencies and a consequent want of suitable measures to bring the food and the medicines within reach of the people.*[132]

The Society of Friends, in its record of its relief operations noted that though distress in Connaught was greater, they had spent proportionately more in Munster because the lack of a community in Connaught made it difficult to organise relief proceedings,[133] while Board of Works officials were themselves aware of the financial burden facing the poorer areas. The barony of Burrishoole in Mayo, for example, initially applied for £80,000, a sum which was almost three times the area's rental of £23,388. Officials estimated that to employ the district's labouring families at 1/- per day for 80 days would cost £23,388.[134]

It is easy to condemn the British government's relief programme of the autumn and winter of 1846-7 as a misguided, perhaps even malevolent scheme, the consequence perhaps of undue dedication to restricting government intervention in the market-place, but this is too simplistic. Public works were a tried and trusted remedy for famine times, and they had apparently not been unsuccessful in other years. If the numbers applying for relief had been limited to 50 or 100,000, the system might perhaps have coped. However the sheer enormity of the tragedy was not immediately realised and so the numbers who would flock to relief schemes were underestimated. Three-quarters of a million people, one-third of the able-bodied male population was simply excessive. The removal of so many workers from the farm labour force inevitably wrought havoc on the economy, just as the failure of the potato crop had done. No section of the economy — wages, food prices, the structure of agricultural production, — remained untouched. The major distortion which the potato failure brought to the Irish rural economy had neither been foreseen, nor could it have been readily prevented. In September 1846 when the second potato failure was already known, Irish Chief Secretary, Labouchere, who is generally credited with adopting a reasonably sympathetic approach to Irish famine relief problems wrote to the lord lieutenants of the Irish counties outlining his general approach to relief

> The sale of meal or other food in small quantities to persons who have no other means of procuring it, and at the prices of ordinary years, the abstaining from giving higher wages than are paid; or exacting a small quantity of work in return that is required on the works carried out by the Government, the limitation of the works in all cases to the extent to which private employment proved not to be available, these appear to be the chief rules which should be adopted by the Relief Committees for their guidance.[135]

Talk of maintaining wage levels, of doling out food in small quantities, suggests a minor tragedy which would only require marginal alterations to normal practices. It could be argued that in 1846 the total economic basis of rural Ireland had been undermined. Dependence on private employment was utterly foolhardy, both because of the total disruption of price/wage relationships which had taken place, and because it presupposed a greater degree of social responsibility among Irish landowners and larger farmers than in fact existed.

Superficially a more active government food policy would appear to have offered a better solution. However, as already noted, 1846 was a year of general food scarcity and this would have made a repeat of Peel's scheme very difficult, as would the fact that Irish destitution was much greater than in the previous season. Only a free food policy available to almost all comers — such as operated in the summer of 1847 — would have met the circumstances of the total potato failure and it can be argued that it took the harsh lessons of the winter of '46 to persuade the British government to take such a step.

Not surprisingly Ireland during the famine years appeared to many to be ripe for social revolution. One of Peel's first responses to news of threatened famine in 1845 was to draft a coercion bill because he felt that food scarcities would inevitably lead to unrest. Kevin B.

Nowlan remarks, that 'In fact, however, the famine years were to prove conspicuous for their tranquility rather than their turbulence'.[136] This is perhaps something of an overstatement. Agrarian crime rose during 1846, mainly attributable to labourer and farmer unrest as labourers reneged on pledges to pay for conacre land which had yielded only diseased potatoes. Food riots and food thefts during the famine years were of 'an unprecedented character'. Crops such as turnips were lifted from fields, beasts were also stolen, forcing some Cork farmers to sit up at night to guard their crops.[137] Some attacks on boats carrying grain in the Limerick area were also reported. Many contemporaries felt that a total breakdown of law and order was in prospect. Whig Chief Secretary, Henry Labouchere, saw his primary responsibility

> to be to protect the trade in food. There is a good deal of it in the country but it never will be brought freely to market as long as this system of terror prevails.[138]

However, another contemporary observer tended to place the reported food thefts in context, admitting that while there was some plundering of wheat stacks, 'in most such cases the farmer is paid by the party 1/6 per stone for his wheat; thus affording to the farmer a fair remuneration though of course not equal to the market price'.[139]

The relief works provided other outlets for crime. Payment of the workforce in cash brought unprecedently large sums of money into remote areas and afforded easy opportunities for many armed robberies. The decision by the Whig administration in the autumn of 1846 to substitute payment by task for a flat payment provoked several gatherings of men who threatened violence if the existing payments system was not maintained. Access to relief employment proved another area which was fraught with tension. This report from Co. Cork is typical of many:

> On the 10th instant, a party of about 200 men went to the new road making at Courtmacsherry and demanded employment, which being refused, they obliged all the other men engaged on the work (about 80) to leave it, saying that as they were not employed, they would prevent any others from working on it.[140]

Public works officials who failed to give in to such pressures faced threats to their life; several stewards and overseers suffered assassination attempts, notably in the Limerick and Clare areas. The forces of law and order appear to have faced difficulties in dealing with such threats. There are undoubted undercurrents of terror in the comments of many rural-based observers in the autumn of 1846. One Clare commentator wrote

> Every man of rank, and property, person and priest are afraid to do or say anything that may be contrary to the wishes or feelings of the mob, for such the assemblages must be considered to be who crowd into and surround the sessions house.[141]

Reports of unrest would appear to have dwindled as the winter progressed. In the autumn months workers faced a threat of hunger but were still in a position to be agitated by their conditions; as food prices accelerated and access to food became more difficult, political militancy gave way to a more immediate struggle for survival with most of the depleted energy being devoted to obtaining food. This is a common feature of genuine famine conditions. In Russia in the years 1918-22 it was estimated that searches for food occupied up to 70-95% of famine victims' time. In Leningrad during the German siege of 1941-2 the most obvious characteristic of the starving population was its apathy, a description which is also applied to the population of the Dutch provinces which experienced famine conditions as a result of German retaliation in 1944.[142]

Soup Kitchens

Having become convinced that public works were ineffective in coping with the famine crisis the British administration decided to abandon them, replacing them with food depots which would supply cooked food, mostly soup, free to the destitute population and at a low price to others. Cooked food was favoured rather than uncooked meal for a number of reasons. Evidence from relief workers in rural Ireland had already indicated that many families were apparently incapable of successfully cooking Indian meal, despite instructions. Hunger pangs drove many to eat any food given to them raw, or undercooked, with consequential health problems. Of equal importance was the fact that rural Ireland would seem to have suffered from a turf scarcity during famine years because workers had abandoned the normal routine of the rural calendar either for employment on relief works or to search for food. Cooked food also had the ideological benefit of being virtually immune from pilferage, or financial speculation. Unscrupulous traders could not corner the market in bowls of soup or plates of porridge as it was alleged that they had attempted to do with supplies of meal.

The decision to feed a high proportion of the Irish population without charge and without requiring them to enter the workhouse marked a definite break with the famine relief policies of both Peel and the Whigs, who had always insisted on the necessity of not providing gratuitous relief. It also breached one of the canons of the 1838 Poor Law Act which determined that, unlike the English Poor Law, Irish unions would not grant any outdoor relief. Its acceptance indicates that the British government was not as inflexible as some commentators have suggested. Faced with the evidence from officials throughout rural Ireland of the ineffectiveness of public works and the apparent efficacy of the soup kitchens operated by the Society of Friends, they shifted their position. Unfortunately the establishment of soup kitchens took time and required the formation of yet another administrative apparatus. In the intervening period many people starved. Public works continued in operation, reaching their peak employment level of 734,000 in early March, but, on 20 March, 20% of those employed were discharged and dismissals continued at a steady pace through the following weeks.[143] Pending the establishment of soup kitchens many destitute families were suddenly thrown on the poor law. This hiatus in famine relief in the early months of 1847, during one of the most difficult periods of all, and one marked by extremely high death-rates, is probably one of the most serious inadequacies in the whole government relief programme. Paradoxically it was a time when public works *might* have proved effective if the population had retained sufficient physical vitality. By the spring of 1847 the international food crisis was over and food imports flowed into Ireland in ever increasing amounts. Food prices reached their peak in January 1847; by March Indian meal which had been over 2d per lb. was now 1.5d; by August it was under 1d, below the price level of the winter of 1845-6.[144] The wages paid on public works would probably have been sufficient to feed a family again by the late spring of 1847 — if work had been available and men capable of working. In practice relief works were winding down, while the disarray of Irish agriculture meant that farmers had severely curtailed their employment of labour.

Instead it was decided to temporarily implement a system of soup kitchens to be administered by local committees pending an extensive re-organisation of the poor law. A Dublin-based commission was established to oversee the new policy. While the commission could advance loans to speed up operations the ultimate cost of the feeding services was to be placed on the local poor rates. To implement this administrative change new relief committees, organised on the basis of poor law unions rather than parishes—as had been the case with committees handling relief works—had to be established. They generally consisted of local magistrates, poor law guardians, the highest local rate-payers and a clergyman of each persuasion.[145] This again took some time. While the decision to wind up public works was taken in January, food kitchens were not in widespread operation until the late spring and early summer. By 15 May committees had been established in 1,248 of the 2,049 electoral divisions in the country, and a further 600 were established in the following two months. The peak of feeding operations occurred in mid-August when over 3m. people were being fed each day by the state.[146] In all, the relief commissioners advanced over £1.7m. in loans for the running of soup kitchens during the summer of 1847, but these loans were to be repaid in full from local rates. Like public works, soup kitchens relied very heavily on local initiative, with local landowners, clergy, their families or other benevolent citizens being responsible for organising the soup boilers.

Society of Friends

While the soup kitchens were being organised the mass of the rural poor was dependent either on the poor law or on private charity, notably the relief efforts of the Society of Friends. The role of the Society of Friends in Irish famine relief has been justly appreciated by even those most critical of British policy during those years. Charitable organisations, both in Ireland and in Britain, had contributed much in the form of famine relief to Ireland in previous seasons of distress. The threat of famine in the spring of 1846 provoked the re-establishment of the Dublin-based Irish Relief Association, and bodies such as the General Central Relief Committee. Voluntary subscriptions from places as remote as Calcutta were channelled to Ireland in response to reports of distress. In November 1846, a group of Dublin members of the Society of Friends decided to form a Central Relief Committee which would act in conjunction with co-religionists in other parts of the country and with members of the Society based in London.

The small number of Irish Quakers included within its ranks a disproportionately large number of prosperous and capable businessmen such as the Pim family, who were heavily involved in textiles, banking and railways, or the Bewley family with interests in the food trade. They brought to famine relief a dedicated compassion, combined with a genuine lack of interest in proselytisation and considerable business acumen. They also had the advantage of close links with English, and indeed American co-religionists, similarly philanthropic and prosperous communities which provided access to substantial funds, and in the American case, generous supplies of cheap food. Food shipments from the American Society of Friends provided almost two-thirds of all Quaker relief supplies. Quaker relief efforts were characterised by considerable emphasis on obtaining accurate information about actual conditions: co-religionists living in provincial Ireland were used, as were travelling investigators and reporters, notably the Norfolk Quaker, William Forster, and Yorkshireman James H. Tuke, both of whom toured distressed parts of Ireland during early months of 1847.

The Society's relief efforts relied heavily on the existence of disinterested and capable expertise. Their reports, and the account of James H. Tuke, continually lament the lack of a middle class in many parts of Ireland and their report admits that Connaught got less relief assistance than might have been expected because the middle class to oversee disbursement was lacking. The Quakers sought out 'reliable local agents' who were provided with 'small and frequent grants' for dispersal. Initially grants were only given to supplement local efforts.[142] The Dublin Committee was also characterised by a relatively cautious attitude towards relief, an unwillingness to interfere with the social and economic order, or to criticise the government. At an early stage they decided therefore to concentrate on

> those cases for which sufficient provision had not been made by Government or which did not properly come under its care, and which had not been relieved by the operations of other associations.

They were wary of providing food free of charge and determined on a policy of providing free boilers and money grants to local committees to purchase food which would be cooked and sold at a very cheap price, generally in the form of soup. The deteriorating conditions of Ireland in the winter of 1846-47 caused the London Friends' Committee to urge them to adopt a more active, and more extensive policy of relief; in particular the latter body suggested that free supplies of food should be shipped to the most distressed areas. However the Dublin Friends still retained their cautious attitude. They decided that it would not be appropriate to compete with private merchants who should be left as the main market suppliers. Hence they were prepared to ship rice, which was not ordinarily handled by Irish traders, but not grain.

The Friends' soup kitchens were of primary importance in the spring and early summer of 1847. The Society offered to operate soup kitchens throughout all the most distressed unions, pending the establishment of government soup kitchens, provided that the government pay 50% of the cost, but the offer was rejected. In the light of the undoubted physical and emotional exhaustion of most committee members by the end of 1847, one wonders if they would have been capable of carrying out their offer. Once the government soup kitchens were in operation by June 1847 they scaled down their efforts, thinking 'it right to withdraw as far as possible from gratuitous issues of food'.[148] They continued to supply clothing, but concentrated most of their remaining efforts on helping the sick and the elderly, primarily on promoting fishery development, supplying agricultural seed, encouraging flax cultivation and other long-term improvement schemes. Proposals that they should re-establish soup kitchens during the winter of 1847-48 were considered and rejected, so too was Trevelyan's offer of £100 if they would again become active in the summer of 1849. In their report, their reluctance to resume relief activities is justified, not without reason, by the sheer physical exhaustion of committee members. However it also reflects the undoubted conservative ideologies of the Dublin committee. Gratuitous almsgiving was viewed as inherently damaging, in particular because it might interfere with government arrangements to deal with the poor — particularly through the poor law.

It seems obvious both from comments in the Society's records of relief operations, and from the contrasts between the account of the west of Ireland published by English Quaker, James H. Tuke, and the opinions of Jonathan Pim, secretary of the Dublin Committee, that the English representatives tended to be more radical in their proposals, and also more critical of the social structure of Ireland. Thus Tuke in his account provided fundamental criticism of the landlord and tenant system and argued that in the western part of Ireland the poor law system was utterly incapable of tackling the problems which existed, while the report of the Dublin Committee both urged that relief be left to the government, and rejected any proposed reform of land legislation — such as fixity of tenure — as a 'violation of the rights of property'.[149] Without dismissing the value of the Society of Friends activities, it might also be worthwhile placing them in context. They provided almost £200,000 — the majority of this in food provided by American Friends which was shipped across the Atlantic free of charge by the British government. In contrast the British government, through loans and grants for a range of purposes, including drainage and land improvement during the famine years, spent over £10.5m., while government soup kitchens during the summer of 1847 cost over £1.7m.

Poor Law and Famine Relief

The establishment of an Irish poor law system in the year 1840 was explicitly designed to meet long-term needs of the Irish poor but *not* to deal with a major famine. This remained the initial reaction of the British authorities with the onset of famine in 1845 when the only role apparently envisaged for the workhouses was in the provision of fever hospitals. Thus the famine relief apparatus established by Peel ignored the existence of the poor law, though when Russell reorganised the system in the autumn of 1846 the chairman of each local poor law board was appointed to the local relief committee. The initial impact of famine on the workhouses was slight. By March 1846 when food was becoming scarce there were only 51,000 inmates in Irish workhouses, approximately 50% of capacity.[150] The sharp rise in food prices in the winter of 1846-7 and the obvious inability of public works to cope with distress placed increasing pressure on the poor law system, while the sharp escalation of food prices and the near unavailability of potatoes meant rising feeding costs and necessitated changes in diet. By Christmas 1846, 56 workhouses were overcrowded and within a month there were 108,487 inmates in workhouses which had been built with a total capacity of 100,000. Those in the more distressed areas of the west and south-west faced the most serious pressure. Faced with grave local distress, lack of space and a heavy demand for relief, many poor law boards of guardians, particularly in the Cork area, resorted to providing outdoor relief in the form of food supplies despite the fact that such relief was expressly forbidden by the 1838 act. It would seem that many poor law unions adopted the practice of gratuitous food relief several months before it was officially authorised and introduced by the government in the summer of 1847.[151] The example of disobedient boards of guardians may have been as influential in persuading the government to introduce soup kitchens as the better known Quaker precedents. For many families the poor law rather than the Quakers bridged the gap until the establishment of the soup kitchens in the summer of 1847. Certainly workhouse numbers, which remained in excess of 100,000 from January until July 1847, showed a fall during the second half of June, when the soup kitchens were fully operational and continued to decline until early September, shortly after the cessation of the soup kitchens, when they had reached 75,376.[152]

Soup kitchens had been established in 1847 as a purely temporary provision pending the full-scale reform of Irish poor relief which was implemented in August 1847. Under this measure a separate Irish Poor Law Commission, independent of the English body, was established for the first time, while the existing poor law unions were re-organised and their number increased from 130 to 163, Many of the very large unions in the west of Ireland were sub-divided and new workhouses erected. In marked contrast to the original intention, the poor law was now given primary responsibility for famine relief, through both indoor and outdoor relief. By the autumn of 1847 it would seem, without being unduly cynical, that the novelty of Irish famine was wearing thin and it was increasingly being seen as a permanent rather than a temporary problem. Hence the attraction of a permanent solution. Despite the persistence of famine conditions—there was another major potato crop failure in 1848 and a lesser one in 1849 and conditions of unusual distress persisted in Ireland until the early 1850s—there were no further famine relief committees, no public works, no special independent soup kitchens. Even the activities of voluntary agencies such as the Society of Friends had been sharply scaled down. Relief was now available only after recourse to the poor law guardians who would provide assistance, either inside or outside the workhouse. Outdoor relief was normally to be limited to those suffering from old age, long-term illness or disability, or widows with two or more dependent children, though such relief could be extended to other categories if no space could be found in the workhouse. During 1847 and '48 many workhouses erected temporary accommodation, or opened auxiliary premises to meet the pressure of demand and many workhouses were permanently extended to meet what appeared at the time to be a long-term need.

Workhouse inmates included all sections of the population but a disproportionate number were women and children. Many of the women were genuine widows, but others had been abandoned by a husband; some children were orphans, but others had been abandoned by both parents, either temporarily or permanently. In some instances parents left children in the workhouse intending to collect them or send for them from America when economic circumstances permitted. Many remained a long-term burden on the poor law. Already by February 1847 children under fifteen years, though some would have had parents in the workhouse, constituted a majority of all workhouse inmates; they also constituted a majority of inmates in 1851. The poor law guardians were forbidden to take children without first ascertaining that they had been orphaned, and many women and children gained admission only by making false declarations of orphancy. In other cases the whole family entered the workhouse but the parents then absconded, leaving their children behind. This was such a major problem at Kanturk workhouse that the surrounding walls were raised to 13 feet to prevent surreptitious exits by abandoning parents, but some still managed to escape.[153]

Numbers in receipt of poor law assistance rose each year until 1849 when they peaked. Dependence on the poor law was further exacerbated by the large-scale failure of the potato crop in the summer of 1848 and by the increasing resort of landlords to eviction. While most of those in need were given outdoor, rather than indoor, relief the balance gradually shifted towards relief in the workhouse as more accommodation became available. As a result of further reforms in 1849 no part of a poor law union was to be more than seven or eight miles from a workhouse, in marked contrast to the position in 1846 when areas such as Erris were more than forty miles from the nearest workhouse.[154] Whereas in the year ending 1847 a total of 417,139 were relieved in the workhouse, this had risen to 610,463 in 1848 and 932,284 in 1849. Numbers receiving outdoor relief, however, peaked at 1,433,042 in 1848, falling to 1,210,482 in the following year. In 1850 they fell even more sharply, and by 1852 outdoor relief was being granted only to a small minority of cases.[155] The increasing reliance on indoor, rather than outdoor, relief also reflected the attitude of poor law guardians, though this varied considerably in different areas. Guardians in Ulster were generally loath to grant outdoor relief and by 1849 it was either totally unknown, or extremely rare in many northern unions. In other areas, however, the increasing reliance on indoor relief reflected the impact of both eviction and the Gregory clause — so called from Sir William Gregory M.P. for Dublin, whose widow, Lady Augusta Gregory, was subsequently to achieve fame for her role in the Anglo-Irish literary revival. This clause, which was passed in August 1847, denied public relief to all holding more than one-quarter acre of land. In an effort to evade its operations, land-holders engaged in fictitious leasing of land to more affluent friends or relatives; others attempted to evade its imposition by placing their wife and children on poor relief while themselves remaining in occupation of the family holding, a practice prohibited by the poor law.[156] Many were undoubtedly forced to give up their land to gain relief and lost their homes in the process. It is impossible to assess the numbers forced into the workhouse by the Gregory clause.

It probably only worked to intensify an already-strong tendency towards eviction on the part of Irish landlords faced with crippling rates burdens and a mass of destitute tenants who were heavily in arrears. Evictions left many in the workhouse with no alternative home. When Kenmare board of guardians attempted to transfer some of its inmates to outdoor relief they refused because they had nowhere else to go as their homes had been levelled.[157] With overcrowding in workhouses, many who sought admission were turned away. James H. Tuke in his travels in Connaught in the autumn of 1847 wrote of Swineford Union

> On 10 November 120 were admitted beyond the regulations and hundreds were refused admission for want of room. Some unhappy beings perished on the high roads and in the fields.[158]

Some who were receiving outdoor relief because of lack of space in the workhouse had lost their homes through eviction, and the poor law commissioners noted families in receipt of outdoor relief being forced to part with some of their scanty food allowance in return for accommodation.[159]

The placing of the burden of continuing famine relief on the shoulders of the poor law system reflected the long-standing belief of Trevelyan and other authorities that Irish poverty should be the responsibility of Irish property. He felt that it was desirable 'to make the burden as near local as possible in order that it may be locally scrutinised and locally checked'.[160] However, localisation almost invariably meant bankruptcy, or near bankruptcy in many localities. The English Quaker, James H. Tuke, who toured the west of Ireland in 1847, was adamant that whereas in most of Ireland there were sufficient resources for the burden of poverty to be locally borne, this was not the case in Connaught, Donegal, or parts of Kerry, Limerick and Clare.[161] Tuke's assessment proved correct. There had been resistance to the poor rate and difficulties in collection in some parts of the west even before the famine. Once famine struck the cost of poor relief escalated, as did the poor rates. By 1847, for example, the guardians of Westport Union were levying a rate of 10/- in the £. In many instances, however, the levy became an almost academic exercise. Small farmers were virtually destitute, rent arrears were mounting, many of the middling and larger farmers who might have been in a position to pay rates resisted paying up. In many instances the high burden of rates induced farmers to sell their stock and emigrate with their families. The problem was exacerbated by the fact that the heaviest burden of poor relief, hence of rates, was in the poorest unions whose populations were least able to pay. Not surprisingly many unions became technically bankrupt, unable to pay their bills or to repay loans from the Dublin administration while some refused to strike a rate. A total of 33 boards of guardians were dissolved between August 1847 and March 1848 and replaced by vice-guardians who were public servants. The dissolved boards of guardians included virtually every union along the western seaboard south of Sligo and many inland western unions, plus a number of more surprising instances such as Athlone, Granard and Mullingar. In general, however, dissolution coincided with areas of acute distress, suggesting that local circumstances rather than mis-management was responsible for financial difficulties. In many instances the replacement vice-guardians did not prove notably more successful in curbing expenditure.[162]

The poor law was left to handle the continuing distress caused by recurrent famine, cholera and other medical disasters virtually without outside assistance. A re-establishment of public works was mooted early in 1848 but rejected by Trevelyan, though James H. Tuke felt that it might be desirable to at least complete the many road works left unfinished in the spring of 1847.[163] While still contending with serious distress they were forced to begin the almost impossible task of repaying the government loans granted for relief during 1846 and 1847. By February 1848 all but six unions had struck a rate for the repayment of government loans.[164] Kerry landlord, Sir John Benn-Walsh, recounted a conversation in 1849 with the vice-guardian of his local union, a Mr. Flood.

> The picture he draws of the union is frightful. Since last year the debts have increased eightfold (despite having a vice-guardian in control). There are now 22,000 paupers on outdoor relief out of a population by the last census of 78,000 now probably 10,000 less. He estimates that there are not potatoes to feed the people three months even if the crop be good, and the blight has re-appeared in many parts. The vice-guardians have already collected all the produce of the butter in rates and they are prepared to strike another in September to secure the produce of the harvest. The fact is that the landed proprietors are now the mere nominal possessors of the soil. All the surplus produce is levied by the Poor Law Commissioners.

Such heavy impositions, at a time when scarcity was still recurring, increased the regional economic problems and hindered possibilities of recovery. Benn-Walsh lamented in 1849, 'My estate offers the singular spectacle of great prosperity, improvements and progress as far as the tenants and state of the land is concerned, yet neutralized by all the exactions of the government and of the poor rates'.[165] A poor law inspector from Ballina Union in 1848 reported 'large tracts of land remaining unproductive', because of the 'broken-down state of the majority of landlords' and tenants lacking the resources to stock and cultivate their land.[166]

The only relief to over-burdened unions came from the British Relief Association, a charitable organization which used the funds it collected in both Britain and America to meet some of the cost of feeding school children in the distressed unions of the west of Ireland. They assisted in the maintenance of up to 200,000 children in both 1848 and 1849.[167] Those responsible for poor law administration, either in Dublin or in rural areas, were forced to manage a system whose rationale many strongly questioned. The Poor Law Commissioners appointed inspectors to many western unions to oversee administration, report on incompetence and generally improve efficiency. However the inspector appointed to Ballina Union wrote

> The question must now be determined whether the experiment of making property support poverty is to be continued in the west of Ireland and I have no doubt whatsoever such an experiment must ultimately fail and I therefore think it would be most cruel to persevere in it.

Appeals to the British treasury for financial assistance for the distressed unions proved unavailing, despite the plea of Twistelton, an Irish Poor Law Commissioner

> I want to leave distinctly on record that, from want of sufficient food, many persons in these unions are at present dying or wasting away; and at the same time it is quite possible for this country to prevent the occurrence there of any deaths from starvation by the advance of a few hundred pounds.[168]

The only response to these pleas was a decision that a levy of 6d in the £ would be placed on the rates in the more prosperous Irish unions, producing a maximum sum of £100,000 which would be transferred to relieve the distressed unions. The establishment of a separate Irish Poor Law Commission had probably made it impossible to consider extending the levy to British unions. In fact, many of the more prosperous Irish unions, especially those in Ulster, strongly objected to the charge.[169] The extreme localisation of the poor rates burden led to acute pressure on the part of ratepayers to divest themselves of as much of the burden as possible. Erris was established as a separate union, partly because of the need for workhouse accommodation closer to an area of acute distress than the Ballina workhouse, which was forty miles distant, but the reform did have the advantage of relieving Ballina ratepayers of the burden of maintaining one of the most deprived areas in Ireland. With the re-organization of poor law units in 1849 there was considerable manoeuvring on the part of landlords to ensure that their estate was not linked for rating purposes with an area containing a large destitute population. Benn-Walsh reported meeting a Limerick merchant who had within the past two or three years purchased a 'considerable estate' which was now being formed by those determining poor law boundaries 'into an electoral division to itself' which would mean that the landlord would have his poor rates burden 'within his control' as he would only be responsible for maintaining paupers from his own estate. Benn-Walsh himself made a point of going with his agent to meet those determining poor law boundaries in his area and he reported with apparent relief that under the new arrangements his estates 'would be thrown with better partners than at present'[170] presumably reducing his long-term burden.

Famine Deaths

For most people the Irish famine is synonymous with massive mortality. Estimates of the numbers who died have varied widely in the range from 500,000 to one million people. The mortality statistics of the 1851 census, which suggest almost one million deaths in total, including 'normal' and famine deaths for the years 1846-51, are undoubtedly an underestimate as they rely on the recollections of survivors to record family deaths. This process is rather hazardous in normal circumstances; given the disruption of the famine years, when whole families died out and others emigrated, it is undoubtedly seriously defective. Estimates for excess deaths during the famine years must take as their starting point the 1841 population, that of 1851, and an assumed 'normal' death rate. Those who have otherwise 'disappeared' can be deemed to be famine victims, or to have emigrated. The range of possible deaths can therefore vary, depending on whether one assumes famine emigration statistics to be accurate, or not. Low emigraton estimates give rise to a high death rate; higher emigration estimates to a correspondingly lower figure for deaths. Neither death nor emigration figures can be derived without certain fundamental assumptions. Recent work by Mokyr, which broadly accepts the accuracy of famine emigration figures — with some adjustments — estimates that at least one million extra deaths occurred during the famine years. Boyle and O Grada, in a separate, and as yet unpublished, analysis calculate that during the famine years the Irish death-rate doubled.[171]

A regional analysis of famine mortality conducted by Mokyr reveals an uneven incidence. The excess death rate was least in east Leinster, the Dublin area and north-east Ulster. Medium excess death rates occurred in the remainder of Leinster, central Ulster such as Tyrone and Armagh, and in Co. Tipperary, while high excess mortality was registered in most of Munster and south Ulster. The highest death rates occurred in Connaught, particularly in Sligo and Galway, with Mayo undoubtedly the most affected county of all. Mokyr claimed that there was no obvious link between excess mortality and degree of dependence on the potato, perhaps because 'the dependency on potatoes before the famine was so extensive and the destruction of the crops in 1846 so complete that variations in the potato acreage per capita or per acre hardly mattered'.[172] This hypothesis is confirmed by a cursory analysis of the 1848 potato failure which had its greatest impact in the northern midlands, in counties Cavan, Longford, Meath, Monaghan, Dublin, Westmeath and Kildare. Distress however was undoubtedly still concentrated in the west and south-west of Ireland, areas where potato yields in 1848 were above-average, though there was apparently some increasing mortality in the eastern and north midland counties.[173] Income levels, literacy and size of farm emerge from Mokyr's analysis as providing a more accurate indicator of ability to survive the famine. Those with holdings of less than twenty acres proved extremely vulnerable, those with larger farms showed a reasonable possibility of survival. Urbanised areas did not necessarily fare better than rural areas, perhaps because the flight of the destitute and starving to the towns brought infections and overstretched sanitary, food and medical resources in what was at the time a generally unhealthy environment. Urban mortality figures are also somewhat complicated by the cholera epidemic of 1849 which was most severe in the major towns and which must be regarded as a disaster which was independent of the famine.

Mokyr's analysis does not consider the impact of government relief policy on mortality levels. This is among the topics considered in a number of articles by Cousens. While Cousens's estimates of famine mortality have become somewhat discredited, this does not necessarily mean that his analysis should be totally dismissed. In common with Mokyr he emphasises the close link between poverty and high mortality. He also tends to attribute the high death rate of the western areas to the break-down of the poor law system and its inability to cope with the crisis, while arguing that the high level of evictions in counties such as Clare, Tipperary and Roscommon contributed to deaths being higher than might otherwise have been expected.[174]

The analysis of Boyle and O Grada concentrates on the age and sex composition of those who died. Their results reveal that famine deaths were heaviest among the young, especially those under five years, and the old, those over sixty. Excess deaths were much lighter among those aged between ten and sixty. As in the case of Mokyr, Boyle and O Grada's work is dependent upon assumptions about emigration: if more children and elderly people emigrated than the figures suggest the number of young and old who died would be correspondingly reduced. However the Boyle and O Grada pattern of heavy mortality among both young and old is almost identical to that which prevailed in 'normal' pre-famine circumstances, something which reinforces their case. The general impression is that the famine doubled the death-rate for virtually all age groups.[175] It would also seem plausible to suppose that the old and young had the greatest difficulties gaining access to food or relief; they were the least capable of earning their living and were least mobile in the search for food. The rector of Schull in west Cork wrote about 'the aged, who with the young are almost without exception swollen and ripening for the grave'.[176] The young had the least resistance to dysentery or infectious diseases, while typhus, which was extremely prevalent during the famine years, caused many deaths among the elderly because it affected the heart. If correct, the age-specific impact of the Irish famine as outlined by Boyle and O Grada is quite similar to that of the Indian famine of 1943 which killed 'by magnifying the forces of death normally present in the pre-famine period'.[177] Their results also suggest that, whereas in pre-famine Ireland, and indeed in post famine rural Ireland until the 1930s, women had a higher mortality level than men, that trend was altered during the famine years with men at slightly greater risk of dying. This greater vulnerability may be due to the pressure of relief works, particularly for bodies deprived of food, or may simply reflect the fact that men have higher calorie requirements than women and thus faced greater difficulties in coping with scarcity. There is a suggestion in McArthur's account of the reports of the Irish commissioners of health that in most serious Irish fever epidemics men constituted the majority of cases, and presumably of fatalities.[178] The greater vulnerability of men to famine conditions has been recorded in other famines. During the famine in West

Holland in 1944 male mortality rose by 16%, female by 7%, while during the siege of Leningrad in the second world war female mortality increased by less than that of men and peaked three or four months later.[179]

The onset of famine deaths lags behind food scarcity. In the Bengal famine of 1943 more than half the deaths attributable to that famine took place after the year 1943.[180] While the year 1846 was marked by an increase in the admission rate to Dublin fever hospitals, the death-rate during that year does not appear to have occasioned any special concern, and the commissioners of health appointed by the lord lieutenant under the Temporary Fever Act in March 1846, in the expectation of an emergency, were disbanded in August.[181] Cousens, the only writer to date to attempt an analysis of the chronology of Irish famine mortality, suggests a peak in deaths in the spring of 1847, which he attributes to the failure of the relief works programme. This is confirmed by a wide range of contemporary evidence. Reports of fever from various areas led to the re-establishment of the board of health in February 1847.[182] In the catholic parish of Kilmore, in west Cork, deaths in the period September 1846-January 1847 totalled 236; deaths in February 1847 alone reached 211, peaking in March at 411. Deaths in April, though high, showed a definite decline, as did those in May, and by June figures were below those in February. Cousens suggests that the improvement was attributable to the effectiveness of the soup-kitchen scheme, yet in Kilmore the first soup kitchen was not established until May, by which time deaths were already declining.[183] In Dublin the worst of the famine deaths had apparently taken place by February 1848 though matters are somewhat complicated by the onset of cholera towards the end of that year, while Belfast dated the end of its epidemics to September 1848.[184] Elsewhere conditions remained acute, and Cousens has identified a second mortality peak in the year 1849 which was attributable to the second potato failure.[185] The health commissioners were not disbanded until August 1850 which may be taken as marking the formal end of the mortality crisis, though the heavy deaths of the later years tended to be concentrated in the west and south-west, areas characterised by a heavy poor law burden and evictions.[186]

One of the demographic impacts of the famine which has hitherto tended to be ignored is the dramatic fall in the birth rate. On the basis of an examination of parish registers, Boyle and O Grada tentatively suggest that the average number of baptisms during the famine period was just under 70% of the number during the early 1840s; allowing for the falling population this suggests a birth-rate which was 80% of the pre-famine level.[187] The decline in births was unlikely to have been uniform throughout the country. A map presented by Cousens based on an analysis of baptismal registers for the year 1847 reveals declines ranging from over 70% in parts of Kerry to less than 20% in the more easterly counties. The timing of this decline is not certain. In the Schull area 1846 was a peak year for baptisms, though by October in that year they had already dropped sharply in the more prosperous Charleville parish.[188] In the following year, however, baptisms in Kilmore parish in West Cork fell by 85% and they fell by 60% in two adjoining parishes.[189] The decline reflected both a sharp drop in the marriage rate and a drop in fertility of married women. Marriages declined due to a lack of surplus income for non-essential purposes and growing apathy towards all activities which were not essential to survival. Evidence from other famines shows an undoubted decline in fertility, though the fertility decline lags behind the decline in food supplies. During the severe wartime famine in Leningrad there was almost total infertility, while in the Dutch famine of 1944 births at the peak of the famine fell to one-third of the expected level, with the impact of infertility being greatest on the poor. Famine would also have resulted in lower average weight of babies born, with consequentially higher deaths and probably some increase in congenital abnormalities, particularly spina bifida. However, follow-up studies of those born during the Dutch famine suggest that those surviving the early months of life suffered no long-term impact.[190]

Irish famine victims died from a variety of causes. Only a small minority of deaths can be directly attributed to starvation. The 1851 census returns of those dying in the previous ten years recorded 20,402 deaths from starvation and 22,384 from 'dropsy' — which was undoubtedly hunger oedema — the swelling of organs as a result of acute starvation. Cousens argues that this probably underestimates the number of deaths from starvation. Those dying of fever often died in institutions; people starved to death alone, but even if the true figure is double or treble that recorded, deaths from starvation remain the exception rather than the norm in famine mortality. Deaths from starvation and oedema were undoubtedly concentrated in the most deprived localities. The rector of Schull — an area of acute distress — wrote of local victims 'swollen and ripening for the grave'. The other ailment which can be directly attributed to dietary deprivation is scurvy, which is caused by an insufficient supply of vitamin C. This disease was almost unknown in pre-famine Ireland due to the high consumption of potatoes. Already by the summer of 1846 the condition was very common in Mayo and Galway, beginning first with ulcerated mouths, developing later in fatal haemorrhages. The dispensary doctor in Ballygar, Co. Galway, recorded it as the first medical consequences 'of the potato failure.[191]

The overwhelming majority of famine deaths, however, occurred from typhus, relapsing fevers and dysentery. The relationship between food deprivation and fever is rather imperfect. Victims of anorexia, for example, are not at increased risk from fevers. There were no widespread fever epidemics in Germany in 1945-6 despite serious undernourishment, while the Netherlands also escaped epidemics during its famine of 1944-5.[192] Dysentery, though an infectious disease, bears some relationship to food deprivation, as unsuitable food and inadequate diet can make people more liable to infection. Many Irish famine accounts describe victims eating maize which was inadequately cooked — it required pre-soaking and long boiling before consumption; or eating raw turnips or other available sustenance. Some doctors attributed dysentery to the eating of seaweed, shellfish or incorrectly cooked Indian meal.[192]

Typhus and relapsing fever, however, are both carried by lice and bear no direct relationship to starvation. This is confirmed by the fact that typhus in particular was responsible for the deaths of many doctors, clergymen and others in presumably comfortable circumstances during the famine years. Typhus, relapsing fever, and dysentery owe much, however, to dirt. Elizabeth Smith in a characteristically censorious comment attributes the spread of dysentery to 'dirty habits, dung-heaps at door, stagnant pools', and more sympathetically 'the inability to buy soap this year'.[193] One Kilkenny doctor wrote of the famine which 'reduced the physical and moral energies of our people to the lowest standards, engendering unwonted habits of filth and vagrancy, which scattered in all directions the seeds of disease which drove people to the towns leading to overcrowded lodgings and accumulated filth'.[194] Typhus was apparently endemic in Ireland. During the famine years its incidence spread because of greater filth and overcrowding. Surplus clothing and bedclothes were invariably disposed of to raise some food. Rev. N. McEvoy, parish priest of Kells, Co. Meath, wrote of

> our famishing countrymen who during the late spring and present summer have pawned for food to prolong existence their last wretched rag of daily as well as of nightly clothing: thanks to God, many and many an Irish pastor is now sleeping upon a bed 'no longer his own' through his sympathies for his suffering flock.[195]

Virtually all accounts of famine victims speak of their rags. The Society of Friends devoted much effort to providing supplies of clothing to remedy these needs. However, even when spare clothing was available, shortages of soap, lack of energy to draw extra water, plus the lethargy resulting from lack of food meant that cleanliness suffered. This is common in many famine situations. Accounts of the Russian famine of 1922 mention indifference to personal cleanliness. Lice were extremely common in Auschwitz concentration camp as a result of chronic overcrowding and lack of water.[196] Irish conditions were undoubtedly aggravated by a shortage of fuel. The wet weather of 1846 made turf harvesting difficult, while the diversion of workers to relief schemes coupled, probably, with the lack of energy for taxing work meant that many simply did not bother to save fuel. Scarcity of turf increased the tendency for the poor to huddle together which facilitated the spread of lice. The movement of population from one area to another, the congregation of people, on relief works and at soup kitchens, plus the chronic overcrowding in workhouses, hospitals and emigrant ships all facilitated the spread of fevers. Areas previously immune were infected by the arrival of strangers; beggars frequently spread the disease in other instances. The disease was brought to the east by the shift of population in search of food and work. In this respect remoteness of location was a positive advantage. The islands of Inishbofin and Inishark off the Mayo coast, despite suffering from potato failure and a shortage of fish, remained free from fever until the summer of 1848.[197]

Prevention of these epidemics was virtually impossible, given that they were inextricably bound up with the total disruption of food supplies, work practices and lifestyles. The precise cause of fever and the mode of transmission of disease were not properly understood, and this undoubtedly hindered efforts at prevention. To exhort people to pay greater attention to personal hygiene when they lacked food would have been ineffectual, while the best efforts at hygiene by workhouses and fever hospitals crumbled in the face of chronic overcrowding and a desperate shortage of money and manpower, which often led to the death or severe illness from fever of those in charge. One answer was to prevent overcrowding by refusing admission. Thus the Dublin fever hospitals rejected more than half of those who applied for admission in the summer of 1847,[198] but such a regime only resulted in the sick dying on the roadside. Extra fever beds were provided, often in auxiliary sheds erected in the grounds of the workhouse, but many lacked bedding and soon became overcrowded in turn.

Mortality was heaviest from typhus, a disease which apparently was particularly severe on more prosperous people. One in thirteen of the 473 medical officers appointed to special fever duty died during the famine, many from typhus. Their high mortality, and that of magistrates, clergy and others in comfortable circumstances, is partly attributed to their often being middle-aged or elderly. Typhus damaged the heart and affected the elderly more severely; children escaped relatively lightly. While many of the poor had acquired partial immunity to the disease from earlier infections, this was less likely among the middle and upper classes. Children on the other hand were more likely to have died from dysentery. Many children, particularly those in workhouses, suffered from ophthalmia, an eye infection which spread rapidly in dirty overcrowded conditions. In the years 1849 and 1850 a total of 41,000 cases occurred in Irish workhouses, the vast majority among children, and over 1,000 lost their sight totally or partially in the process.

Emigration

Excess deaths accounted for only approximately half of the population losses incurred during the 1840s. Many who did not die emigrated. Emigration to North America rose somewhat in 1845, more sharply in 1846 and doubled in 1847. Its peak however was in the years 1851 and 1852; thereafter it fell back considerably. Figures for emigration to Britain are less reliable. The British Census of 1841 records 419,256 Irish-born living in that country; by 1851 it had risen to 733,866 and the Irish constituted 3½% of the total population, their highest level ever. Mokyr estimates that there were approximately 420,000 emigrants during the decade 1841-51, the majority presumably during the famine years.[199]

Traditional accounts of emigration have regarded the famine as marking a major break with both earlier attitudes and patterns. Oliver McDonagh states that 'the blight had totally reversed the peasant's attitude to emigration' and rejects the opinion that 'it was no more than the pre-famine exodus writ large'. He sees the famine emigration as containing a large 'element of hysteria', 'something which was more a headlong scrambling from a stricken area, more a flight of refugees, than an emigration as ordinarily understood'. He sees peasantry faced with want and misery, left 'in an unstable condition, ready to be swept by some mass sentiment', and provides an account of the famine exodus which suggests that it was highly irrational.[200] There is undoubtedly some degree of truth in this account. The famine years brought autumn and winter emigration for the first time—

something which undoubtedly worsened travel conditions. Some embarked without any supplies for the journey. However, given existing conditions in Ireland, it could be argued that emigration was among the most rational responses. This is particularly so of the numbers of strong farmers, men of 20 acres or more, and businessmen, such as bacon merchants, who were apparently well represented among the emigrants of 1847. They had not left during the first potato failure. However, faced with continuing famine which meant an almost total collapse of trade for many businessmen dependent on the rural market, and the prospect of crippling taxes on all save the smallest landholders, many preferred to liquidate their capital, selling livestock and crops and taking their families with them to America. For many the alternative was using the same assets to pay rent arrears or taxes in Ireland. The emigration of these solid farmers with their families aroused considerable consternation among contemporary observers. It would seem that their number has been exaggerated. O Grada has discovered that over 60% of emigrants to New York during the years 1847-8 were servants or labourers, a figure almost identical to their proportion in the previous decade, though McDonagh sees the year 1849 as marking the peak of prosperous emigration.[201]

Nor can the emigration of the poor be dismissed as an irrational move either. The hazards and uncertainties of an Atlantic crossing undoubtedly seemed preferable to the options open in Ireland of unemployment, life in the workhouse, at worst death. For many the only deterrent was the lack of funds. Some Irish landlords, such as Monteagle, lobbied the government in 1846 to embark on a programme of assisted-emigration as part of their famine relief package, but, as in the past, the idea was dropped largely because of fears of the costs involved and the need to assume responsibility for settling emigrants in their new homes. The only state assistance to emigration during famine years involved the shipping of 4,000 female orphans from Irish workhouses to compensate for a scarcity of women in Australia. Landlord initiative was more active and approximately 22,000 emigrants (only about 5% of the total number) had their emigrant fares paid by landlords who realised that this provided the most humane and efficient way of ridding their estates of paupers and in the process reducing their poor rates. Such initiatives were patchy, but very significant on estates where they were adopted, such as the Gore-Booth estate at Sligo.[202] For Kerry landlord, Sir John Benn-Walsh, assisted emigration became an integral part of his policy of estate re-organization. Tenants in arrears, cottiers, those holding small patches of land in rundale or partnership holdings, were induced to give up their land and emigrate; the resulting holdings were consolidated and used to increase the land-holding of efficient tenants or to create new larger farms.[203] By 1849 or 1850 such measures had become increasingly attractive to landowners in the west and south-west, areas which bore the heaviest poor-rates, when a once-off emigration charge was compared with long-term maintenance in the workhouse. In the year 1851 Lord Lansdowne spent £14,000 on emigrant fares for all the paupers who were charged to his estate.[204] Landlord initiative caused some boards of guardians to follow suit. They were permitted to borrow on the rates to finance emigration passages and thousands of workhouse residents emigrated to British colonies from 1849.[205]

Only a small minority of famine emigrants were assisted in this manner. The majority were forced to find the necessary amount to pay for their passage, or they depended on remittances from earlier emigrants to pay their way. Price was therefore a critical consideration for most emigrants, and they sought the cheapest possible means of crossing the Atlantic. Emigrants often walked across Ireland to Dublin or east-coast ports where they embarked for Liverpool, the city which offered the cheapest fares, rather than set sail from an Irish port. It was cheaper to travel to Canada than to the United States because Canadian vessels were subject to less regulation, so Canada became the most common destination. Once arrived those who were in fit condition walked across the border into the United States.

No account of famine emigration would be complete without reference to coffin ships. The death-rate on some ships was more than fifty per cent. Mortality was often higher among newly-arrived emigrants than at sea. Among emigrants to Canada in 1847 over 5% died at sea; 3.46% in quarantine on Grosse Isle and over 8% in Canadian hospitals.[206] Deaths resulted from a variety of factors: some were due to unsuitable ships crossing the Atlantic, often in mid-winter in an effort to cash in on the heavy demand for emigrant passages. The majority, however, were not caused by shipwreck, but by outbreaks of fever — generally ship fever on board. Many accounts emphasize the lack of food, the severe overcrowding and the insanitary conditions on board, but, as McDonagh shows, mortality in several instances was worse on some well-equipped and supervised vessels than on inadequate ships.[207]

Many of those emigrating during the famine times were the truly destitute. Those assisted to leave by landlords, for example, were generally the poorest and those least capable of managing a farm. They were therefore thoroughly ill-equipped in all senses to cope with emigrant travel. Dirt and lack of sanitation, which posed major health problems on land during the famine years, were even more intractable at sea. Emigrants often travelled without adequate clothing; what they had was already ragged and dirty. Hygiene standards were low and more difficult to maintain in crowded ships where water and washing facilities were scarce. Cheap passages often provided little in the way of food and many famine emigrants lacked the funds to bring their own. In fact, as on land, dirt appears to have been the major liability. Ship fever, like typhus and relapsing fever, was borne by lice. Mortality was apparently heaviest on ships embarking from large ports such as Liverpool. Many emigrants spent days or weeks before travelling in overcrowded lodging-houses and were already incubating fevers when they embarked. In the confined quarters they infected most of the passengers during the journey. While preventing such catastrophes might have been possible, it would have proved extremely difficult. The horrors of famine crossings, particularly in 1847, gave rise to tighter legislation controlling emigrant ships in the future, but requirements that there be a ship's doctor on board would have proved relatively useless when faced with the mass of lice-bearing, fever-ridden passengers which constituted an all too large number of Irish famine emigrants. Emigrant ships, no less crowded, arrived from other European countries during these years, but with comparatively insignificant death-rates, because other emigrants had not suffered the degree of destitution or exposure to fevers which characterised the Irish.

While the emigration of the famine years undoubtedly brought new peaks to the earlier trend and gave rise to unprecedented horrors, it would now seem that famine emigration should be seen not as marking a dramatic break with earlier trends, but as constituting considerable continuity. Emigration was already rising rapidly in the years before the famine and Cormac O Grada's analysis of emigrants reaching New York during 1847-48 leads him to conclude that they differed 'less markedly from those who preceded them in the late 1830s and early 1840s than might be expected'. Famine deaths occurred disproportionately among the young and the old; the majority of those emigrating were young adults, though more emigrants were aged either under fifteen or over thirty-five than in the past, and while Ulster still accounted for the lion's share, 40.6% in 1847-8 compared with 36.7% in the years 1835-46, the proportion from Connaught almost doubled from 12.9% to 24.2%.[208] The heaviest levels of emigration during the 1840s occurred from the north midlands and the north-west, from counties such as Mayo, Roscommon, Sligo, Leitrim, Longford, Cavan and Monaghan. High, though lesser, emigration took place from Galway, Clare, Tipperary and more southerly midland counties. This pattern suggests a shift to the south and the west of the traditionally strong Ulster emigration which was already well established in counties such as Sligo before 1841 and also tends to confirm continuity in patterns rather than a break.

Evictions

One of the least attractive aspects of the famine years is the comparatively high level of evictions which took place, a process which undoubtedly intensified human misery. The decades prior to the famine were characterised by the attempted restructuring of estates in an effort to consolidate farms and reduce the pressure of population. However, the full vigour of consolidation was apparently thwarted by the threat of agrarian violence and perhaps by landlord indifference. The famine intensified the pressures in favour of restructuring. The sharp rise in the cost of labour led to a decided increase in cattle numbers and a reduction in tillage acreage which was not to be reversed. The repeal of the corn laws in 1846 may have been read by many large farmers as marking increased uncertainty in grain markets. Of more importance, perhaps, famine deaths and emigration gave more breathing space on many estates. For the first time in perhaps a century landlords were faced with vacant holdings and the possibility of some restructuring. In many instances, however, deaths and emigration did not give sufficient breathing space, while the famine intensified the pressure on landlords to reduce their tenant population by forcible means. The famine marked an undoubted crisis for many landlords. By 1843 an estimated one thousand estates, accounting for a rental of over £700,000, one-twentieth of the rental of the country, were in the hands of receivers. This figure increased to £1,300,000 by 1847 and £2m. by 1849.[209] Rent arrears during the early famine period do not seem to have been excessively high; Elizabeth Smith reported a high level of receipts during 1846,[210] but continuing famine undoubtedly led to steadily growing arrears, particularly among the hard-hit small farmers. For larger farmers and landlords the greatest burden came from taxation. The decision to charge the cost of most famine relief schemes to local taxes meant that all middling and large farmers, those with holdings valued in excess of £8, were faced with crippling levels of taxation. In the case of smaller holdings the cost was borne by the landlord.

This left landlords whose estates contained a substantial number of smallholdings with a double incentive to remove such tenants. Small tenants were probably the least likely to pay their rent and the most likely to become dependent on famine relief, while eviction combined with consolidation, by reducing the number of small farms, could ease the landlords' tax burden. The problems faced by surviving middlemen were probably greater than those facing landlords. The decades prior to the famine posed difficulties for some of this class,[211] difficulties much increased during the famine years. Much middlemen property was sub-let in very small holdings to the class of tenant least likely to cope with the failure of the potato crop. Whatever sympathy landlords may have shown to tenants in arrears did not extend to middlemen, and their financial difficulties proved an ideal opportunity for some landlords to end their lease.

While eviction statistics prior to 1849 pose certain difficulties, it would appear that in the early years of the famine they remained low. There were 4,599 actions brought for ejectment (excluding those relating to city properties) in the year 1846. We do not know how many of these were successful, but the success rate in subsequent years was 75-80% and this suggests a probable ejectment figure in the region of 3,500-3,600 families. In subsequent years the level rose; to 6,026 in 1847; 9,657 in 1848. In 1849 a total of 16,686 families were evicted; this peaked at 19,949 in 1850 and declined to 13,197 in 1851, falling sharply during the remainder of the 1850s.[212] These figures marked the peak of Irish evictions, but even in 1850 they constitute only 2.5% of the total number of agricultural holdings.

The impact of these evictions was probably magnified by their localisation. The years 1846-8 were marked by relatively heavy eviction levels in the Ulster counties of Armagh, Antrim and Monaghan. Cos. Leitrim and Tipperary also experienced relatively high levels with Leitrim suffering the highest rate in the country. In 1849 and 1850 evictions, while rising, became more localised, with Munster, notably Tipperary, Clare and Limerick, accounting for over 43% of the national total in both years. The proportion of evictions in Connaught also rose somewhat, that in the other provinces declined. While Co. Clare was severely hit by the famine there is no evidence of disproportionately severe impact in Co. Tipperary, the county which accounts for the highest relative level of evictions throughout these years.

The relationship between famine distress and eviction levels is therefore by no means a simple one. The heaviest burden of famine relief on local taxation fell on the counties of the west of Ireland, such as Mayo and Galway. While these areas were by no means immune from eviction the volume was considerably less than in other areas. Nor do evictions appear to have been directly motivated by landlord indebtedness or insolvency. While Co. Tipperary, the county with the highest level of famine evictions, recorded a high level of indebtedness among its landlords prior to the famine, so too did Co. Cavan, which does not feature prominently in the famine eviction statistics. Co. Clare, which does, in contrast recorded a relatively low level of pre-famine landlord indebtedness.[213] The absence of an easy relationship between rent arrears and evictions is further confirmed by government statistics which record that in the years 1846, 1848 and the early months of 1849 the majority of ejectment order were described as due to 'Overholding on the title' — tenants remaining in possession after expiry of a lease rather than to non-payment of rent, though the latter cause accounted for the majority of ejectment orders in the year 1847. 'Overholding', however, suggests landlords motivated to evict in order to consolidate holdings rather than merely pressurised by the burden of insolvent tenantry. Both economists and government inquiries had been urging the need for a more streamlined Irish farming structure in the immediate pre-famine decades. The famine disaster apparently confirmed the merits of their arguments, while increasing financial difficulties may have reduced landlord reluctance to evict. The famine also increased the financial difficulties and reduced the solvency of many surviving middlemen and there is little doubt that many eviction orders were initially directed against this body of men. In these circumstances sub-tenants were also generally removed. Many of the evictions in the notorious Kilrush Union involved such middlemen, and the casualties were large numbers of sub-tenants, the majority holdings less than five acres, some only in possession of a cabin and no land.[214] Many landlords justified such evictions on the grounds that the people in question were not their legal tenants.[215]. In addition, as Beames argues, the famine was marked by a serious erosion of the strength of the agrarian secret societies and this permitted widespread eviction free from the threat of retaliatory action.[216] It may be no coincidence that counties of record eviction levels, such as Tipperary, Limerick, Clare and Leitrim, were among the areas of heavy pre-famine agrarian crime, suggesting that an earlier restructuring process had been hampered by the strength of secret societies. Once these were apparently weakened during the famine, landlords embarked on a series of evictions which had been previously thwarted. Restructuring was apparently a relatively slow process. All counties with above average eviction rates displayed a sharp decline in the number of agricultural holdings. While the total number of holdings in the country as a whole fell by almost 20% between 1847 and 1850, the decline in Clare was double that level and both Tipperary and Limerick reported declines of almost 30%; in all of these counties, however, the increase in cattle numbers was below the national average.

The evictions of the famine years intensified the hardship which many families had suffered because of lack of food and exposure to disease. Cousens argues, probably with some validity, that they were responsible for increasing the death rate in some counties.[217] Evictions imposed a heavy burden on the poor law system, notably in Co. Clare where the evictions of Kilrush Union were the subject of special government inquiry.[218] It can be argued that, peaking in the years 1849-51, when the worst of the famine had passed, they prolonged suffering and distress. They also played a major role in bringing about a restructuring of the Irish agriculture scene. While much of the reduction in smallholdings was brought about by famine deaths and emigration, evictions added a measure of compulsion to be resorted to by landlords who felt that natural wastage had not been sufficient.

The evictions of the famine years have been frequently presented as the norm in Irish landlord-tenant relations and as such they provided potent ammunition for those arguing the injustice of landlord rule. In fact they are the exception rather than the rule. Both prefamine and post-famine evictions levels appear to have been relatively low. It would appear that the prolonged pressure of the famine years broke the normal landlord reluctance to evict and that the cumulative horrors of the preceding years numbed landlord sensitivity to the suffering which they were causing. The official reaction varied. Local poor law officials faced with the human consequences of eviction in the form of workhouses overcrowded with destitute people were naturally critical. Some at Westminster viewed evictions as a necessary preliminary to the introduction of modern scientific farming in Ireland, but in general the government regarded such measures with disfavour even in cases where the estates were hopelessly encumbered. While they favoured consolidation they preferred to see it emerge through voluntary emigration of surplus tenantry.[219] However, it should perhaps be remembered that while tens of thousands of families were evicted, many hundreds of thousands remained undisturbed, many of them surviving on small uneconomic holdings on which they had undoubtedly accumulated arrears. Many landlord families, such as the Martins of Connemara, who were already on the verge of bankruptcy before the famine, chose to support their tenantry and in the process guaranteed the loss of their family estate, and, ironically, the eviction during the 1850s of many of their former tenants under the less benign regime of a new landlord.[220]

Conclusions

The Irish famine was more than a mere crop failure; its ramifications spread far beyond a serious food shortage though the significance of the latter should not be underestimated. The famine years gave rise to a fundamental disruption of many of the key elements in the Irish economy. As a result of the failure of the staple foodstuff of the Irish population food prices soared, giving rise in consequence to the major disturbance of existing wage rates and of the fundamental basis of pre-famine agriculture—the hiring of very large numbers of low-cost labourers or cottiers to participate in a highly intensive if technologically primitive form of agriculture.

Given the degree of disruption caused by the potato failure of 1846, the role of the British government as a relief agent should perhaps be seen in a more sympathetic light than it is generally regarded. Government policy was undoubtedly restricted by ideology—in particular the unwillingness for a long time to distribute free food—but so were the actions of charitable bodies such as the Society of Friends and late-twentieth century world famine relief operations remain no less hide-bound by ideological and economic considerations. In this light it does not appear appropriate to pronounce in an unduly critical fashion on the limitations of previous generations.

Perhaps the major problem which Ireland faced during the great famine was the fact that she had made many earlier appeals to British generosity, both public and private. These had been met, but in the process goodwill was eroded. The fact that earlier crises and indeed the 1845 potato failure had been met with apparent ease by operating a limited scheme of public works, and, in 1845, a restricted government food distribution system, may have blunted the appreciation of the magnitude of the problem which emerged in the autumn of 1846. Criticism is frequently voiced of the failure of the British government to directly intervene in the food market in that year, but the sheer size of the task and fact that it would undoubtedly have led to a boycott of the food trade by private traders made such an action of limited effectiveness.

Government policy can, however, be criticised on a number of fronts. While the chopping and changing of the composition of relief committees, their terms of reference, their geographical boundaries and other matters may have had some rationale in bureaucratic circles, there is little doubt that valuable time and effort was wasted in such matters. Similarly, while the decision to switch from a massive public works programme to a mass feeding programme in the spring of 1847 reflects a measure of pragmatism and a willingness to depart from previous ideological beliefs, the decision to first abandon the relief works and then to set up soup kitchens with the major delay which ensued was deplorable. Public works should have been retained in some form, perhaps on a reduced scale, regardless of their drawbacks, until food kitchens became operational.

The major criticism of government policy, however, must be reserved for the decision to abandon any special famine relief programmes, to deny the continuation of an emergency after the autumn of 1847 despite the fact that distress remained prevalent in Ireland throughout 1849 and in some cases until 1850. This loss of interest was not unique to the government; most charitable agencies suffered a similar lack of stamina, but it suggests a callous indifference to continuing death and suffering once the novelty of the Irish famine had worn off. The absence of special government attention meant that the continuing Irish famine became not just an Irish charge, but a local charge with Erris property bearing the burden of Erris poverty and the administrative burden falling on the newly-established separate Irish poor law, a body specifically not designed to cope with major famine.

In commenting on government attitudes it seems vital to distinguish between officials in Whitehall, notably Trevelyan, and their counterparts in Dublin. The majority of Dublin and rural-based public officials emerge as displaying genuine concern for the problems of the Irish population and most of their reports display a keen appreciation of the broad ramifications of the famine on Irish society. They are thoroughly aware of the long-term consequences of diverting men from their own holdings to public works and suggest a compromise formula whereby men would be paid for relief works while encouraged to spend part of their time working on their own land—a proposal rejected with horror in London. It is easy to see why Trevelyan, Assistant Secretary to the Treasury, has been presented as a major scapegoat for the government's famine policy.[221] His tone of self-righteous moralising smacks of the worst of Victorian ideology. Yet he was only articulating what were commonly-held opinions, while it remains difficult to conclusively argue that greater sympathy with the Irish case would have automatically guaranteed a dramatically reduced mortality.

Any criticism of public response to the famine should not be restricted to the British government and its officials. The response of the Irish public—if we can talk of such a group—was highly ambiguous. Despite the subsequent capitalising on the event by nationalist writers, notably John Mitchel, the experience seems to have paralysed most influential Irishmen at the time. Daniel O'Connell merely relied on his traditional alliance with the Whigs and while his response may perhaps be excused on the grounds that his powers were waning—he died in 1847—there is no strong identifiable call from Ireland for any particular measure to meet the famine. Even the call to prevent food exports was much stronger in retrospect that it was at the time. The inadequacy of the Irish response reflected the lack of political leadership and the strong divisions—both political and sectarian—which prevailed in Irish society at the time. These divisions also weakened the effectiveness of local relief administration and in the process threw a correspondingly greater burden on the over-worked public officials. In the process innocent people undoubtedly died. While the decision of the British government to establish a separate Irish poor law system in 1847, and in consequence to leave the costs of the famine as an Irish rather than a United Kingdom charge, can be criticised on the grounds that it effectively denied the reality of the Act of Union, the unwillingness of more prosperous parts of Ireland to shoulder even a small proportion of the burden of the poorer unions suggests that self-interest was not a British monopoly. In fact, that long-term burden of famine repayments was removed from Ireland in 1853 when Gladstone as chancellor of the exchequer assumed central government responsibility for famine debts and simultaneously harmonised Irish and British tax levels introducing income tax to Ireland for the first time.[222]

The famine must be seen as bringing about a major breakdown of Irish society. Family structures, traditions of hospitality, the practice of basic hygiene all appear to have been temporarily undermined by the catastrophe. Its broad impact must be seen as roughly akin to major wars or other natural disasters. Given such circumstances options such as emigration appear not as irrational, but as highly logical responses. The fact that the disaster lasted for several years strengthened the conviction for many that the future prospects of Ireland were grim and hence the attractions of England or America were correspondingly increased. However the famine did not initiate emigration; while numbers leaving rose sharply there still remains a measure of continuity with pre-famine trends. The high level of evictions may also perhaps be seen as another response to crisis: the reaction of landlords facing financial ruin. For others the famine provided divine confirmation of the warnings of countless economic experts that many Irish farms were indeed impossibly small and hence afforded full justification for implementing a major reconstruction of their estates.

The famine experience does not lend itself to simple conclusions though many writers have hazarded such in the past. For example, it is difficult to decide whether the massive deaths which ensued should be seen as confirming that Ireland was doomed, in the 1840s or somewhat later, to suffer a major subsistence crisis, or whether the famine should not be seen as reflecting extraordinary bad luck. The fact that a high proportion of the Irish population in the 1840s lived in extremely vulnerable circumstances is not in doubt, but five years of major food failure was an extremely heavy burden to bear. Lives could undoubtedly have been saved by more judicious relief management but it is difficult to assess how this might best have been done given the limitations of the 1840s. Finally there remains the ongoing debate as to its long-term impact on Irish society—which further serves to indicate the contradictions in the event.

EPILOGUE: THE IMPACT OF THE FAMINE

There is little doubt that the famine was a significant event in nineteenth century Irish history, but its precise impact is a matter of some considerable debate. The famine has, at one stage or other, been held responsible for almost every subsequent occurrence in Irish history from the decline of the Irish language and an upsurge in religious devotion to sweeping changes in Irish agriculture and the engendering of a strong hostility to England which inevitably led to the movement for national independence. There is little doubt that conditions and attitudes in Ireland changed during the course of the nineteenth century. The population declined; the structure of agriculture was altered, housing conditions improved, diet became more varied, marriages became later and fewer. What is at issue is the extent to which the famine can be held responsible for these changes. Traditional interpretatons have generally regarded the famine as the critical factor though more recent scholarship has come to question certain aspects of the 'watershed' theory, arguing that the post-famine decades merely saw a continuation of trends already set in train in earlier decades and presenting a picture which seems to emphasize continuity instead of the hitherto accepted picture of a fundamental change. As in many other areas of Irish history the conclusions which historians now draw are more tentative than in the past. An earlier certainty has given way to ambiguity, though the recent work by Mokyr may be regarded as an exception to this trend.

We may at least be certain of one change. In the century prior to the famine Irish population quadrupled; in the following century it was halved. Population decline, once begun, was not conclusively reversed until the 1960s. However, there remains the doubt as to whether Irish population might not have stabilised and begun to decline in the middle of the nineteenth century, famine or no famine. On this point we can only speculate, but there is tentative evidence that birth and marriage rates were already falling before the famine and there is absolutely no doubt that emigration had already risen to substantial levels by the early 1840s. In this most central area the catastrophe of the famine would seem to have only accelerated trends which were already in train.

The impact on agriculture is also a matter of some debate.[1] Cormac O Grada's estimates of the structure of agricultural output in the years 1840-45 give little support to the belief that in the post-1815 period Irish agriculture was in the throes of a shift from tillage to cattle farming. Tillage products accounted for two-thirds of agricultural output during those years, whereas his figures for the year 1854 indicate that a significant shift had already taken place with livestock now accounting for half of total output. In addition to the changing composition of output it should be noted that post-famine agriculture was producing approximately 16% less than in 1840-45 — reflecting the loss of one-quarter of its workforce.[2]

This analysis would seem to support the view that the famine marked a turning point in the volume and structure of agricultural output. This case is strengthened by the fact that the famine years did see a significant increase in Irish cattle numbers, as larger farmers apparently adjusted from more labour-intensive tillage farming to raising cattle, though some farmers may have been reacting to the 1846 repeal of the Corn Laws which opened Irish grain farming to unrestricted competition from continental and American producers, making tillage farming considerably less certain than in the past. However, the relative prices for tillage and livestock products cannot account for the dramatic shift in the structure of agriculture in the years immediately following the famine. Price trends for grain products were rather volatile but were extremely buoyant in the year 1854. Paradoxically the item showing the greatest price rise since the famine was the potato crop, yet the volume of the Irish potato crop had fallen by one-half.[3] The persistence of blight and a less prolific supply of labour to manure the crops brought lower yields and less reliable crops.

However, from the late 1850s the message from market prices was unambiguous as livestock prices showed a steady increase while grain prices either fell or remained stable. The percentage decline in corn acreage was greater in the years 1861-71 and 1871-81 than in the decade 1851-61.[4] Much of the decline in the 1860s can be attributed to a succession of disastrous harvests in the sixties, the consequence of freakish weather conditions which spelled financial ruin for grain farming.[5] Previously grain farmers could partly compensate for low yields with high prices; because of the free grain trade which now existed this factor no longer operated. Yields were extremely poor yet prices remained low. International market and price trends, therefore, are probably the key factor in the continuing shift towards livestock farming which took place in the second half of the nineteenth century, though the famine, and particularly the sharp fall in the number of agricultural workers and heavy increase in wage costs, is undoubtedly responsible for the shift from tillage which had taken place by the mid 1850s. Given international agricultural price trends it seems probable that Irish agriculture would have experienced a shift towards livestock by the 1860s, famine or no famine. This tendency was undoubtedly accelerated by the sharp fall in the Irish labour force which increased the attraction of abandoning labour-intensive tillage. The famine would seem to have anticipated and accelerated changes which would otherwise have emerged on a more gradual basis.

The impact of the famine appears most ambiguous in the west of Ireland, the area which undoubtedly suffered most. The demography of the west leads one to question some stereotypical images of the famine. The most devastated area gives little indication of dramatic change in its social practices in response to the disaster. Marriages in the decades after the famine took place at an earlier age and with greater frequency in Connaught than in more prosperous parts of the country. In consequence the birth rate was considerably higher. This discrepancy even applied between east and west Cork with the poorer west recording a much higher natural increase in population in the 1850s and 1860s.[6] The marriage rate in the west does not begin to drop until the 1870s and it is not until the early twentieth century that Connaught no longer records the highest marriage rate in Ireland.[7] In the more remote and isolated areas early marriages appear to have remained the norm for several decades later.[8] Emigration from the west was already quite high in the 1850s and '60s contrary to what used to be thought,[9] but there is some evidence suggesting that this process was already beginning in the early 1840s.

Agriculture in the west also shows much less immediate response to the devastation of the famine years. Despite the seemingly inescapable proof of the potato's vulnerability and strong pressure from so-called experts for crop diversification, potato acreage recovered throughout the 1850s from its immediate post-famine low in the counties of the west and north-west. Thus the area worst affected by the failure of the potato crop consistently records the heaviest post-famine potato acreage and the least shift from tillage to pasture.[10] As late as 1871 more than 60% of tilled land was still under the potato in the Castletown Union of West Cork and in Ennistymon Union in Co. Clare. Several other areas devoted more than 50% of their tilled land to potatoes.[11] If the horror of the famine alone had caused previous trends to be overturned we would expect potato acreage to have fallen most sharply in that area. This suggests that the impact of the famine on Irish agriculture lay not in psychological reaction but in the consequential impact on costs and prices. Labour in the west was family rather than hired labour and so was less affected by rising wage rates. Land for potato ground was obtained not by renting it from increasingly unwilling farmers but by using the family farm or by taking over a plot of waste land which remained plentiful in western counties,[12] while the west proved less adept at increasing livestock investment because of the persistence of small farms and lack of capital.

The famine undoubtedly resulted in the consolidation of farm holdings, though not as significantly as was previously thought. One farm in four disappeared between the years 1845 and 1851, with all of the decline concentrated in the holdings of less than fifteen acres. The average size of farm increased. In 1845 36% of farms consisted of more than fifteen acres, by 1851 the figure was 51% while the percentage of holdings under five acres fell from 24% to 15%.[13] Consolidation was, however, a once-off process, the product of famine deaths and record evictions. Farm numbers and size changed little between 1851 and the first world war.

The turnover among the landlord class was at least as dramatic with the Encumbered Estates Court in 1849 facilitating the speedy sale of bankrupt estates. While indebtedness among Irish landlords was not a new phenomenon, the burden of famine relief and mounting rent arrears seriously worsened the situation. In contrast to the consolidation of farms, which was telescoped into a short time span, the sale of bankrupt estates remained a continuing feature of the second half of the nineteenth century. The Encumbered Estates Court was originally intended to be a short-term institution, but its existence was repeatedly extended throughout the 1850s until, in 1858, it was given permanent status and a new name as the Landed Estates Court.[14] By 1870 the majority of Irish landlords were newcomers, but they tended to have smaller estates and the majority of land was still in the hands of traditional landlord families.

The cottier or labourer class was the major casualty of the famine. They were disproportionately numbered among its victims and those who survived found a continuation of their old lifestyle increasingly difficult. By the 1850s farmers were increasingly reluctant to grant conacre or to permit labourers to erect cabins on their land. This reluctance was a reaction to the famine experience when many labourers reneged on their side of the bargain once their potato crop had failed, and even more to the fact that farmers' rates bills during famine years were burdened with the upkeep of local labourers and their families. Denying land and housing to labourers appeared a useful method of preventing heavy poor rates in the future and this reluctance to house labourers in many rural localities survived into the closing decades of the nineteenth century, extending even to an unwillingness to build government-subsidised labourers cottages in the 1880s and 1890s. Deprived of land and housing and faced with fewer job opportunities because of the switch to cattle and the introduction of mechanical reapers,[15] labourers were forced to emigrate. They constituted a majority of all Cork emigrants in the 1850s.[16]

The decline in the number of labourers and the consolidation of farms meant that post-famine Irish society tended to be dominated by the values, mores and lifestyle of the farmer. More than one-third of all Irish houses in 1841 were one-roomed cabins; by 1861 they constituted less than ten per cent of the housing stock and housing standards continued to rise throughout the remainder of the century. The improvement reflects the disappearance of the labourers and an improvement in housing standards among farming families. Whether this was a new process in the later nineteenth century we do not know, as evidence of living standards for farmers in pre-famine Ireland is negligible. Dependence on the potato declined in the Irish diet, in part because the potato crops in the second half of the century were never as prolific as in earlier years. Blight and some decline in intensive manuring and other traditional practices were responsible for this. By the 1860s the diet of labourers and small farmers had diversified to depend on Indian meal for sustenance during the spring and summer months.[17] The spread of Indian meal was accelerated by the famine but it had apparently been making some inroads in pre-famine years. This meant a decline in food self-sufficiency and an increasing reliance on shops. How much of this trend can be attributed to the famine, how much to the commercial revolution which followed the railways it is impossible to say. Literacy levels rose in 1851 when 42% of men and 51% of women were completely illiterate, compared with 46% of men and 59% of women in 1841 — a reflection, not of a revolution in schooling but of the heavy mortality among the poor and consequently among illiterates. While no comparable figures exist there was undoubtedly a sharp drop in the proportion of Irish speakers for the same reason. The continuation of both trends — increasing literacy and anglicisation — reflect the declining labouring population perhaps as much as they reflect the impact of the national schools. Many of the changes in Irish society which have been attributed to the famine, such as more orthodox religious practices, probably reflect the predominance of farmers and their values at the expense of the labouring community. Some recent writers see the emergence of the farming community to a pre-eminent position as a key element in the land war of the 1880s.[18] Whether such a social transformation would have occurred had there not been a famine is a debatable point. It certainly would not have happened in as swift or decisive a fashion.

Analysis of the long-term impact of the famine is seriously bedevilled by the fact that Irish economy and society after 1850 was significantly different from that before 1850. However, it would be foolhardy in the extreme to conclude, just because of these differences, that all change can be attributed to the famine. Much of the analysis must rest on the perhaps artificial question of whether Irish population would have declined irrespective of the famine. There is little doubt that the decline in population, the falling proportion of labourers and cottiers in the population and the consolidation of the position of the farming community had far-reaching effects. But to attribute these monocausally to the famine is probably unduly simplistic. One of the matters which has received considerable attention in recent years is the changing influence of the catholic church in nineteenth century Irish society. Historians have suggested a shift from a peasant-style native religion in which christian and pagan elements were carefully intertwined — patterns and wakes being among the most noteworthy examples — to a more formally-disciplined and orthodox pattern of religious practice.[19] In the process the catholic clergy, who had preached, often in vain, against traditional superstitions in the pre-famine period,[20] apparently gained a greater control over their flocks. David Miller has argued that this greater clerical authority stems directly from the famine, when the peasantry had recourse to their traditional rituals and found them wanting. The destruction of the French vineyards by pylloxera in the later nineteenth century has similarly been held responsible for the disappearance of traditional religious rituals in many areas.[21] A more plausible explanation in the Irish case would appear to be found in the decline of the Irish-speaking, illiterate, labourer and poor farmer population — the group most attracted to traditional rituals — and the consequent dominance of the mores of the farming community.[22] In fact recent research is tending somewhat to further confuse the picture by suggesting that already before the famine the avalanche of church building and new Roman practices, such as forty-hours adoration, benediction and missions, which characterised the so-called 'devotional revolution', were already well in train, at least in the more prosperous parts of the country.[23]

The political implications of the Irish famine are also beginning to come into question. The conventional wisdom is easily expressed:

the creation of undying hatred which led inescapably to Irish political independence, or maybe even to neutrality in the second world war. Thus Cecil Woodham—Smith's final pages

> The famine left hatred behind. Between Ireland and England the memory of what was done and endured has lain like a sword. Other famines followed, as other famines had gone before, but it is the terrible years of the Great Hunger which are remembered, and only just beginning to be forgotten.
>
> Time brought retribution. By the outbreak of the second world war, Ireland was independent, and she would not fight on England's side. Liberty and England did not appear to be synonymous and Eire remained neutral. . . .
>
> There was also a more direct payment. Along the west coast of Ireland, in Mayo especially, on remote Clare Island, and in the dunes above the Six Mile Strand are a number of graves of petty officers and able seamen of the British Navy and Merchant Service, representatives of many hundreds who were drowned off the coast of Ireland, because the Irish harbours were not open to British ships. From these innocents, in all probability ignorant of the past, who had never heard of failures of the potato, evictions, fever and starvation, was exacted part of the price for the famine.[24]

Robert Kee's television history of Ireland favoured a similar interpretation.[25]

In practice the immediate impact of the famine was more complex. While there was general dissatisfaction with government handling of the crisis and consequential anti-English feeling it did not automatically transmit itself into a demand for independence. Vincent Comerford has written that 'For most observers, including the great bulk of previously 'repealer' opinion, the famine provided not an argument in favour of self-government, but several devastating arguments against it . . . . it shattered the confidence of the repealers in the viability of a self-governing Ireland'.[26] In later years the famine became a potent image to be harnessed to Irish demands for self-government or social reform, but it is only one of many, joined to the image of a steadily falling population, continuing mass emigration and the extinction of Irish industry. A sense of economic injustice was used to fuel the nationalist cause. The famine was only one ingredient in this.

The most potent impact, that on the famine victims, is the most impossible to assess. The extensive survival of recollections of famine times, the food eaten, relief works, deaths and emigration in popular folklore testify to its impact, an impact probably strengthened because it was the last such disaster in Irish life. The personal consequences of the disaster, however, still escape us. For survivors it must have meant the loss of kin — people widowed, orphaned, parents who had lost most, perhaps all of their children. The problem of broken families was intensified by heavy famine emigration. It also meant the destruction of many communities. Deaths, emigration and eviction resulted in the wiping out of small villages or clusters of households. In the process many traditional customs were also disrupted. Many oral accounts see the famine as marking the permanent end to traditions of hospitality and customary pastime.

> It didn't matter who was related to you, your friend was whoever would give you a bit to put in your mouth. Sport and pastimes disappeared. Poetry, music and dancing stopped. They lost and forgot them all and when the times improved in other respects, these things never returned as they had been. The famine killed everything.[27]

Nostalgia for the past is a common feature of oral recollection, but there is little doubt that an early-nineteenth century Ireland with a predominantly young and growing populaton, less constrained by the dictates of late marriages and formal match-making, would have offered more scope for celebration. Yet vestiges of old merrymaking and of offering hospitality to all undoubtedly survived. *The farm by Lough Gur,* an account of life on a large farm in Co. Limerick in the post-famine period records almost indiscriminate hospitality in the kitchen for all travellers, plus occasional, though undoubtedly supervised dances when wandering fiddlers appeared.[28]

The above paragraphs may leave a confused impression of the precise impact of the famine on Irish society. This is probably the correct picture. While it would be a travesty to dismiss the event as of little real significance, it would be equally undesirable to lay every change in Irish politics or society at its feet. The famine cannot be seen in isolation from the changes taking place in Ireland and in western Europe in the preceding and succeeding decades, nor is it the story of a monolithic Irish peasant nation being starved by the prosperous British. It has been claimed that the extraordinarily generous Irish response to the recent Ethiopian famine appeals reflects the potent popular memory of the famine; perhaps the range of information now available on the difficulties and shortcomings of twentieth-century famine relief schemes may lead to a greater understanding of the problems faced during the Irish famine.

REFERENCES

PART 1 (pp 1-6)

[1] K. H. Connell, *The population of Ireland, 1750-1845* (Oxford, 1950).
[2] L. M. Cullen, 'Population trends in seventeenth century Ireland' in *Economic and social review*, vi, 2, (1975), p. 160 supports the higher figure but this is disputed by Nicholas Canny, 'Early modern Ireland: an appraisal appraised' in *Ir. Econ. & Soc. Hist.*, iv, (1977), p. 64.
[3] Stuart Daultrey, David Dickson and Cormac O'Grada 'Eighteenth century Irish population: new perspectives from old sources', *Jn. Economic History*. xli, no. 3, (Sept. 1981) pp. 601-28; also David Dickson, Cormac O'Grada and Stuart Daultrey, 'Hearth tax, household size and Irish population change, 1672-1821' in *R.I.A. Proc.*, 82, C, no. 6, (1982) pp 125-81.
[4] For Irish population change from 1821 to the famine see Joseph Lee 'On the accuracy of the pre-famine Irish censuses' in J. M. Goldstrom and L. A. Clarkson (ed.), *Irish population economy and society. Essays in honour of the late K. H. Connell* (Oxford, 1981) and also Joel Mokyr and Cormac O'Grada, 'New developments in Irish population history, 1700-1850', in *Econ. Hist. Rev.*, xxxvii, no. 4, (Nov. 1984), pp 476-7.
[5] Ibid., p. 476.
[6] J. H. Andrews, 'Land and people c. 1685', in T. W. Moody, F. J. Byrne and F. X. Martin (ed.), *A new history of Ireland*, iii, (Oxford 1976), p. 458.
[7] L. M. Cullen, *The emergence of modern Ireland, 1600-1900* (London, 1981), p. 12.
[8] Ibid., p. 109.
[9] Ibid., p. 96.
[10] Dickson et al. *R.I.A. Proc.* 82, (1982), pp 164-8.
[11] E. A. Wrigley and R. S. Schofield, *The population history of England, 1541-1871: a reconstruction* (London, 1981).
[12] M. W. Flinn, *The European demographic system, 1500-1820*, (Baltimore, 1981) p. 20.
[13] David Dickson, 'A note on Cromwellian transplantation certificates', (unpublished paper, TCD 1982).
[14] D. E. C. Eversley, 'The demography of the Irish Quakers, 1650-1850', in Goldstrom and Clarkson, *Ir. population*, p. 63.
[15] Mokyr and O'Grada, 'New developments in Irish population history', p. 477.
[16] Joseph Lee, 'Marriage and population in pre-famine Ireland', in *Econ, Hist. Rev.*, xxi, (1968), pp 283-95.
[17] Joel Mokyr, *Why Ireland starved* (London, 1983), p. 36.
[18] Ibid., pp 37-8.
[19] Cormac O'Grada, "Malthus and the pre-famine economy' in Antoin Murphy (ed.), *Economists and the Irish economy from the eighteenth century to the present day*. (Dublin, 1984) p. 83.
[20] John D. Post, *The last great subsistence crisis in the western world* (Baltimore and London, 1977).
[21] Valerie Morgan, 'Mortality in Magherafelt in the early 18th century' in *I.H.S.* xix, 74 (Sept. 1974) pp 130-4 and Valerie Morgan, 'A case study of population change over two centuries: Blaris, Lisburn, 1661-1818' in *Ir. Econ. & Soc. Hist.* iii, (1976), pp 14-16.

[22] Dickson et al. *R.I.A. Proc.* 82 (1982) p. 174.
[23] Louis Henry 'The population of France in the eighteenth century' in D. V. Glass and D. E. C. Eversley, (ed.)., *Population in history* (London, 1965), p. 448.
[24] Peter Razzell, 'Population growth and economic change in eighteenth and early nineteenth century England and Ireland' in E. L. Jones and G. E. Mingay (ed.), *Land labour and population in the industrial revolution* (London, 1967) pp 260-81.
[25] Thomas McKeown, *The modern rise of population* (London, 1976).
[26] Dickson et al. *R.I.A. Proc.*, 82 (1982) p. 167.
[27] James Donnelly Jr., 'Irish agrarian rebellion: the Whiteboys 1769-76' in *R.I.A. Proc.*, 83, no. 12 (1983) p. 296.
[28] The issue is complex; see Mokyr and O'Grada, 'Irish population', pp 481-3.
[29] L. M. Cullen, 'Irish history without the potato' in *Past and present*, 40, (July 1968), pp 72-83; for a more recent perspective by Cullen, see 'Population growth and diet, 1600-1850' in Goldstrom and Clarkson, *Ir. population*, pp 89-112. Joel Mokyr, 'Irish history with the potato' in *Ir. Econ. & Soc. Hist.*, viii, (1981), p. 27.
[30] Dickson, et al. *R.I.A. Proc.*, 82 (1982) p. 162.
[31] W. J. Smyth, 'Land-values, landownership and population patterns in Co. Tipperary for 1641-1660 and 1841-50' in L. M. Cullen and F. Furet (ed.), *Ireland and France 17th-20th centuries: Towards a comparative study of rural history* (Paris, 1980) p. 77.
[32] Dickson et al. *R.I.A. Proc.*, 82 (1982) p. 162.
[33] Raymond Crotty, *Irish agricultural production; its volume and structures*, (Cork, 1966) p. 16.
[34] David Dickson, 'Property and social structure in eighteenth century south Munster', in Cullen and Furet, *Ireland and France*, pp 133-5.
[35] L. M. Cullen, *An economic history of Ireland from 1660* (London, 1972) p. 53.
[36] Dickson 'Eighteenth century Munster' p. 136.
[37] K. H. Connell, 'Illicit distillation in Ireland' in K. H. Connell (ed.), *Irish peasant society: four historical essays* (Oxford, 1968).
[38] T. W. Freeman *Pre-famine Ireland* (Manchester, 1952).
[39] Crotty, *Irish agricultural production* p. 21.
[40] Graeme Kirkham "Economic diversification in a marginal economy: a case study" in Peter Roebuck (ed.), *Plantation to partition. Essays in Ulster history in honour of J. L. McCracken* (Belfast, 1981) p. 79.
[41] W. J. Crawford, *Domestic industry in Ireland* (Dublin, 1972) p. 5.
[42] Eric Almquist, 'Pre-famine Ireland and the theory of European proto-industrialization', in *Jn. economic history*, xxxiv, no. 3 (1979) pp 35-71.
[43] Ibid.
[44] Mokyr, *Why Ireland starved*, p. 63.
[45] William Greig, *General report on the Gosford estates in Co. Armagh*, (Belfast P.R.O.N.I., 1976).
[46] Eric L. Almquist, 'Labour specialisation and the Irish economy in 1841: An aggregate occupational analysis' in *Econ. Hist. Rev.*, xxxvi, no. 4 (Nov. 1983) pp 512-513.
[47] W. Nolan, *Fassadinin: Land, settlement and society in south-east Ireland 1600-1850* (Dublin 1979), p. 97.
[48] David Dickson, 'Middlemen' in Thomas Bartlett and J. Hayton (ed.), *Penal era and golden age* (Belfast 1979), pp 162-85.
[49] Dickson, 'Eighteenth century south Munster' p. 135.
[50] For changes in leasing patterns see W. A. Maguire, *The Downshire estates in Ireland, 1801-45* (Oxford, 1972), pp 110-112 and Peter Roebuck 'Rent movement, proprietorial incomes and agricultural development, 1730-1830' in Roebuck (ed.), *Plantation to partition.* pp 91-9.

51 W. H. Crawford, 'The social structure of Ulster in the eighteenth century' in Cullen and Furet (ed.), *Ireland and France*, p. 123.
52 Maguire, *Downshire* pp 121-3.
53 Donnelly, *Cork*, p. 14.
54 Maguire, *Downshire* p. 40.
55 Roebuck 'Rent movement, proprietorial incomes and agricultural development, 1730-1830', p. 40.
56 D. McCourt, 'The decline of rundale' in Roebuck (ed.) *Plantation to partition*, p. 126.
57 William Tighe, *Statistical observations relating to the county of Kilkenny* (Dublin, 1802), p. 268.
58 Greig, *Gosford estates* pp 59-60; cf. Introduction by David Tierney.
59 Issac Weld, *Statistical survey of Co. Roscommon* (Dublin, 1832), p. 255.
60 Greig, op. cit. p. 152.
61 W. J. Smyth, 'Land-values, landownership and population patterns in Co. Tipperary for 1641-1660 and 1841-50' in Cullen and Furet (ed.), *Ireland and France*, p. 77.
62 Mokyr, *Why Ireland starved*, p. 24.
63 Peter Solar, 'Agricultural productivity and economic development in Ireland and Scotland in the early nineteenth century', in T. M. Devine and David Dickson (ed.), *Ireland and Scotland, 1600-1850* (Edinburgh 1983), p. 77.
64 Mokyr, *Why Ireland starved*, p. 19.
65 Michael Beames, *Peasants and power: the Whiteboy movement and their control in pre-famine Ireland* (Brighton, 1983), p. 18.
66 Almquist, 'Labour specialization and the Irish economy', p. 517.
67 Dickson, 'South Munster', p. 135.
68 Cullen *Econ. hist. Ire. since 1660*, p. 118.
69 Dickson, 'South Munster' p. 136.
70 Donnelly, *Cork*, p. 17.
71 Crawford, *Domestic industry*, p. 40.
72 Donnelly, *Cork*, p. 46.
73 Raymond Crotty, *Irish agricultural production: Its volume and structure* (Cork 1966), p. 37.
74 Ibid., p. 276 and J. M. Goldstrom, 'Irish agriculture and the great famine', in Goldstrom and Clarkson (ed.), *Ir. population*, p. 160.
75 Peter M. Solar, 'The agricultural trade statistics in the Irish railway commissioners' report' in *Ir. Econ. & Soc. Hist.*, vi (1979), p. 35.
76 Donnelly, *Cork* p. 28.
77 K. H. Connell, 'The colonization of waste land in Ireland, 1780-1845' in *Econ. Hist. Rev.*, iii, no. 7 (1950), pp 44-71 and P. M. A. Bourke, 'The agricultural statistics of the 1841 census of Ireland, a critical review', *Econ. Hist. Rev.*, xviii, no. 2 (Aug. 1965), pp 390-1.
78 Cormac O'Grada, 'Irish agricultural output before and after the famine', *Jn. European Econ. Hist.*, 13, no. 1 (Spring 1984), pp 151-2.
79 Solar 'Agricultural productivity', p. 81.
80 Maguire, *Downshire*, pp 22 and 32.
81 David Large, 'The wealth of the greater Irish landowners, 1750-1815', *I.H.S.* xv, no. 57 (March 1966) pp 21-46.
82 Mokyr, *Why Ireland starved*, p. 93.
83 Michael Kenny, 'The structure of agriculture in east Westmeath'; unpublished M.A. thesis, N.U.I. (U.C.D.), 1974.
84 Cullen, *Emergence of modern Ireland*, pp 47-50.
87 Maguire, *Downshire*, p. 71.

[88] Cormac O'Grada, 'The investment behaviour of Irish landlords 1850-75: Some preliminary findings', *Agricultural history review*, xxiii (1975), pp 139-55.
[89] *Gosford*, Thompson intro. p. 9; Donnelly, *Cork*, p. 70.
[90] *Report H. M. Commissioners of Inquiry into the state of the law and practices in respect of the occupation of land in Ireland*, 1845, xix, app. li, pp 30-33.
[91] McCourt 'Rundale', p. 138.
[92] Mokyr, *Why Ireland starved*, p. 114; Crotty, *Irish agricultural production*, p. 36.
[93] Kenny, 'East Westmeath' pp 9-10.
[94] Mokyr, *Why Ireland starved*, p. 129.
[95] Kenny 'East Westmeath' p. 20.
[96] Donnelly, 'The Whiteboys' in *R.I.A. Proc.*, 83 (1983), pp 293-4. For a wide range of secret societies see Samuel Clark and James Donnelly Jr. (ed.), *Irish peasants, violence and political unrest, 1780-1914* (Manchester, 1983).
[97] Joseph Lee, 'Patterns of rural unrest in nineteenth century Ireland: a preliminary survey', in Cullen and Furet (ed.), *Ireland and France*, pp 223-4.
[98] Mokyr, *Why Ireland starved*, p. 137.
[99] P. O'Donoghue 'Causes of the opposition to tithes, 1830-38' in *Studia Hibernica*, no. 5 (1965), pp 7-28.
[100] E. P. Thompson, 'The moral economy of the English crowd in the eighteenth century' in *Past and present*, 50, (Feb. 1971), pp 76-136.
[101] Michael R. Beames, 'Rural conflict in pre-famine Ireland: Peasant assassinations in Tipperary, 1837-47', in *Past and present*, no. 81 (Nov. 1978), pp 75-91.
[102] Mokyr, *Why Ireland starved*, p. 132.
[103] Lee 'Patterns of rural unrest' in Cullen and Furet, *Ireland and France* pp 223-237.
[104] Kenny 'East Westmeath' p. 37.
[105] David Fitzpatrick 'Class, family and rural unrest in nineteenth century Ireland' in P. J. Drudy (ed.), *Irish studies 2: Ireland: Land, politics and people* (Cambridge, 1982), pp 37-75.
[106] Conrad Gill, *The rise of the Irish linen industry* (Oxford, 1925) p. 267.
[107] Kenny 'East Westmeath' p. 112.
[108] Timothy P. O'Neill, 'Poverty in Erris', unpublished paper, June 1983.
[109] Gill, *Linen industry* p. 323.
[110] Graeme Kirkham, 'Economic diversification in a marginal economy: a case study', in Roebuck (ed.), *Plantation to partition*, pp 64-81.
[111] *First report of H. M. commission of inquiry into the condition of the poorer classes in Ireland*, 1835 (369), xxxii, App. H. p. 9. (henceforth *Poor inquiry*).
[112] Joel. Mokyr, 'Irish history with the potato', *Ir. Econ. & Soc. Hist.*, viii (1981), p. 11.
[113] *Poor inquiry* App. H. p. 11.
[114] Mokyr, *Why Ireland starved*, p. 12.
[115] Donnelly, *Cork*, p. 20.
[116] Kenny 'East Westmeath' p. 94.
[117] *Poor inquiry, Third report*, 1836 (43) xxx; for Stanley's critique see *Second report of George Nicholls Esq. on poor laws Ireland*, 1837-8 (104), xxxviii, App. No. No. 13.
[118] *Poor Inquiry*, App. H p. 12.
[119] O Grada, 'Irish agricultural output before and after the famine', pp 151-5.
[120] Connell, *Population*, pp 81-2.
[121] Patrick Hickey, 'A study of four peninsular parishes in West Cork, 1796-1855', unpublished M.A. thesis, N.U.I. (U.C.C.), (1980), pp 75 and 96.
[122] Cormac O Grada, 'Prefamine Dublin's demography: the evidence from the Rotunda records', paper presented at the Economic and Social History Society of Ireland Conference, Cork, Sept. 1982.

[123] Phelim P. Boyle and Cormac O Grada, 'Fertility trends, excess mortality and the great Irish famine', unpublished paper, University of British Columbia, 1982.
[124] Post, *Last great subsistence crisis*, p. 97.
[125] W. F. Adams, *Ireland and Irish emigration to the new world from 1815 to the famine*, (New York 1967, first edition 1932), pp 70-1 and 111.
[126] Ibid., pp 159-60.
[127] Cormac O Grada, 'Across the briny ocean', in Devine and Dickson (ed.), *Ireland and Scotland*, p. 118.
[128] Adams, op. cit., pp 94, 162.
[129] Mokyr, *Why Ireland starved*, p. 134.
[130] Adams, op. cit., pp 181-2.
[131] Ibid., p. 142.
[132] Brenda Collins, 'Irish emigration to Dundee and Paisley during the first half of the nineteenth century' in Goldstrom and Clarkson (ed.), *Irish population*, p. 202.
[133] O Grada, 'Across the briny ocean' p. 121.
[134] Adams, op. cit., pp 120-1.
[135] O Grada, 'Across the briny ocean' p. 121.
[136] Adams, *Irish emigration* p. 104.
[137] For Irish emigration in general, see David Fitzpatrick, *Irish emigration, 1801-1921*, Studies in Irish economic and social history, no. 1, (Dublin, 1984).
[138] Collins, 'Irish emigration'.
[139] Adams, *Irish emigraton*, p. 125.
[140] Ibid., p. 209.
[141] Connell, *Population*, p. 145.
[142] Post, *Last great subsistence crisis*, pp 114-5.
[143] Cormac O Grada, 'Malthus and the pre-famine economy', in Antoin E. Murphy (ed.), *Economists and the Irish economy from the eighteenth century to the present day* (Dublin, 1984), p. 83.
[144] Mokyr, *Why Ireland starved*, p. 37.
[145] Timothy E. O'Neill, 'The state, poverty and distress in Ireland, 1815-45', unpublished Ph.D. thesis N.U.I., (U.C.D.), 1971, pp 8-45.
[146] Ibid., pp 78-9.
[147] Timothy P. O'Neill, 'The famine of 1822', unpublished M.A. thesis, N.U.I., (U.C.D.), 1965, pp 44-52.
[148] O'Neill, 'The state, poverty and distress in Ireland' p. 87.
[149] O'Neill, 'Famine of 1822' p. 97.
[150] Hickey, 'Four peninsular parishes in West Cork' pp 78, 87, 91.
[151] O'Neill, 'Famine of 1822' pp 72-3.
[152] R. B. McDowell, *The Irish administration 1801-1914* (London, 1964), pp 166-8.
[153] Connell, *Population*, p. 200.
[154] Oliver McDonagh, *Ireland: the Union and its aftermath* (London, 1977), ch. 2.
[155] O'Neill, 'Famine of 1822', p. 21.
[156] Desmond Bowen, *The protestant crusade in Ireland, 1800-70* (Dublin, 1978), p. 83.
[157] Desmond Bowen, *Souperism: myth or reality?* (Cork, 1970), p. 154.
[158] Ibid., p. 12.
[159] R. D. Collison Black, *Economic thought and the Irish question, 1817-70* (Cambridge, 1960), pp 112-3.
[160] Ibid., p. 22.
[161] O'Neill, 'The state, poverty and distress in Ireland', p. 114.
[162] Ibid., p. 292.
[163] Ibid., p. 133.

[164] Collison Black, *Economic thought*, pp 101-2.
[165] McDowell, *Ir. administration*, p. 204.
[166] Collison Black, *Economic thought*, p. 174.
[167] Ibid., p. 192.
[168] *Second report of the commissioners appointed to consider and recommend a general system of railways in Ireland* 1837-8 (145), xxv.
[169] Kevin B. Nowlan, 'The political background', in R. Dudley Edwards and T. Desmond Williams (ed.), *The great famine* (Dublin, 1956), pp 159-61.
[170] *Poor inquiry, third report*, section IV.
[171] Ibid.
[172] Collison Black, *Economic thought*, p. 176.
[173] Adams, *Irish emigration*, p. 167.
[174] Collison Black, *Economic thought*, p. 213.
[175] Ibid., p. 209.
[176] *Poor inquiry, third report*, section IV.
[177] Hickey, 'Four peninsular parishes' p. 208.
[178] *Remarks of G. C. Lewis on Poor Laws, Ireland* 1837 (90) vol. li.
[179] *Poor inquiry, third report*, p. 25.
[180] Ibid., p. 5.
[181] Collison Black, *Economic thought*, p. 100.
[182] Ibid., p. 107.
[183] *First report of George Nicholls, Esq. on poor laws, Ireland.* 1837 (69) li, p. 4.
[184] Collison Black, *Economic thought*, p. 110.
[185] *First report*, p. 38.
[186] O Grada, 'Malthus', in Murphy (ed.), *Economists and the Irish economy*, p. 80.
[187] Mokyr, *Why Ireland starved*, p. 51.
[188] Ibid., p. 64.
[189] F. J. Carney, 'Pre-famine Irish population: the evidence from the Trinity College estates' in *Ir. Econ. & Soc. Hist.*, ii (1975), pp 35-45.
[190] David Dickson, 'Famine in Ireland, 1700-1775: A review', paper read to conference of Economic and Social History Society of Ireland, Derry, September 1981.
[191] O Grada, 'Malthus', p. 82.
[192] O'Neill, 'The state poverty and distress in Ireland', p. 133.
[193] Ibid., p. 9.
[194] Quoted in Sir William Wilde, *Census of Ireland 1851. Part V. Table of deaths*, p. 214.
[195] Salim Rashid, 'The policy of laissez-faire during scarcities' in *Economic Journal*, 90, (September 1980), pp 498-9.
[196] *Poor inquiry*, 1835 (369), xxxii, Suppl. 2, app. B, part II.
[197] Ibid., app. E.
[198] P. M. A. Bourke, 'The use of the potato crop in pre-famine Ireland' in *Statistical and social inquiry society of Ireland, journal*, xxi pt. 6 (1968), p. 93.
[199] Joel Mokyr, 'Uncertainty and prefamine Irish agriculture', in Devine and Dickson, op. cit. p. 93.
[200] O Grada, 'Malthus', p. 84.
[201] *Poor inquiry*, app. E., p. 17.
[202] Cullen, 'Irish history without the potato' in *Past and Present*, 40, (1968) pp 72-83.
[203] *Poor Inquiry*, App. A. 1836 (369), xxxii, Pt. I, p. 356.
[204] Ibid., p. 361.
[205] Ibid., p. 381.

PART 2 (pp 53-61)

[1] W. Steuart Trench, *Realities of Irish life*, (London, 1869), pp 101-2.
[2] M. Bergman, 'The potato blight in the Netherlands and its social consequences (1845-1847)' in *International review of social history*, 17, pt. 3 (1967) pp 391-431; Joel Mokyr, 'Industrialisation and poverty in Ireland and the Netherlands' in *Journal of interdisciplinary history*, x, no. 3 (1980) pp 981-1008.
[3] P. M. A. Bourke, 'The weather and the great Irish famine', seminar paper delivered University College Dublin, 1982.
[4] Thomas P. O'Neill, 'The organization and administration of relief, 1845-52', in Edwards and Williams, *Great famine*, p. 210.
[5] 'Return showing proportion of actual crop lost', published in *Correspondence explanatory of the measures adopted by her Majesty's government for the relief of distress arising from the failure of the potato crop in Ireland*. 1846, (736) xxxvii, p. 36.
[6] P. M. A. Bourke, 'The extent of the potato crop in Ireland at the time of the famine' in *Statistical and social inquiry society of Ireland, journal*. xx, pt. 3, (1959-60), pp 1-35.
[7] *Correspondence from July 1846 to January 1847 relating to the measures adopted for the relief of distress in Ireland*. 1847 (761), li.
[8] *Poor inquiry*, app. E.
[9] *Reports of the poor law commissioners for 1847* App. A, no. VIII, report, Capt. Sir Thomas Ross, R. N. Dingle.
[10] *Returns of agricultural produce in Ireland, in the year 1847*, 1847-8 (50-II), xlvii.
[11] Calculated from *Returns of agricultural produce in Ireland, in the year 1848*.
[12] Bourke, 'Extent of potato crop' p. 11.
[13] A. Sen, *Poverty and famines, an essay on entitlements and deprivation* (Oxford, 1981), p. 58.
[14] Bourke, 'Use of potato crop in pre-famine Ireland'.
[15] John Mitchel, *The last conquest of Ireland (perhaps)* (Dublin, 1873), p. 208.
[16] P. M. A. Bourke, 'The Irish grain trade' in *I.H.S.* 20, no. 78 (1976) p. 165.
[17] Tom Harper, 'Entitlements during the Irish famine', unpublished M.A. thesis, N.U.I. (U.C.D.) 1983, p. 6.
[18] Bourke, 'Irish grain trade', p. 165.
[19] *Relief of distress*, 29 Aug. 1846. D. Corneille to Trevelyan.
[20] R. M. Barrington, 'The prices of some agricultural produce and the cost of farm labour for the past fifty years, *Statistical and social inquiry society of Ireland, journal*, ix, (1886), pp 137-53.
[21] E. Margaret Crawford, 'Indian meal and pellagra in nineteenth-century Ireland', in Goldstrom and Clarkson (ed.), *Ir. population*, pp 115-118.
[22] Harper, 'Entitlements', p. 16.
[23] David Thomson and Moyra McGusty (ed.), *The Irish journals of Elizabeth Smith, 1840-50*, (Oxford, 1980), p. 103.
[24] *Transactions of the central relief committee of the Society of Friends during the famine in Ireland in 1846 and 1847* (Dublin, 1852), App. III
[25] *July 1846 to January 1847 relief of distress*, Capt. Hutcheson, 19 Dec. 1846.
[26] *Society of Friends*, p. 158.
[27] Thomson and McGusty (ed.), *Irish journals of Elizabeth Smith*. p. 90.
[28] Ibid., p. 104.
[29] *Correspondence from January to March 1847, relating to the measures adopted for the relief of distress in Ireland*. Board of works series (part II), 1847 (797), lii, 8 Jan. 1847.

[30] *Society of Friends*, p. 154.
[31] Ibid., App. III, 13 Dec. 1846.
[32] Ibid., p. 184, 10 Feb. 1847.
[33] *Correspondence, Jan. March 1847 relief of distress*, 7 Feb. 1847.
[34] *Society of Friends*, p. 109.
[35] *Correspondence, Jan. Mar. 1847, relief of distress*, 9 Jan. 1847.
[36] *Society of Friends*, p. 159.
[37] Ibid., p. 53.
[38] *Irish journals of Elizabeth Smith*, p. 131.
[39] Donnelly, *Cork*, p. 131.
[40] Ibid., p. 73.
[41] *Relief of distress*.
[42] Sir Charles Trevelyan, *The Irish crisis*, (London, 1850), p. 4.
[43] *Relief of distress* Knaresborough to Redington, 8 Dec. 1846.
[44] Ibid., Lt. Inglis, Co. Limerick, 19 Dec. 1846.
[45] Ibid., 28 Oct. 1846, Jones to Trevelyan.
[46] *Correspondence, Jan. to March, relief of distress* 30 Jan. 1847, Lieut. Downes.
[47] Calculated from *Returns of agricultural produce in Ireland in the year 1847. Part I*. 1847-8, (923), lvii, *Part II. Stock*. 1847-8, (1000), lvii, 109. *Returns of agricultural produce 1850*.
[48] *Relief of distress*, Low to Jones, Timoleague, 5 Dec. 1846.
[49] *Correspondence, Jan. to March, relief of distress*, Jones to Trevelyan, 16 Feb. 1847.
[50] P. M. A. Bourke, 'The agricultural statistics of the 1841 census of Ireland: a critical revlew' in *Econ. Hist. Rev.* xviii, no. 2 (Aug. 1965).
[51] Trevelyan, *Irish crisis*, p. 4.
[52] *Irish journals of Elizabeth Smith*, 3 May 1847, p. 142.
[53] Trevelyan, *Irish crisis*, p. 71.
[54] Bowen, *Protestant crusade*, p. 179.
[55] A. R. G. Griffiths, 'The Irish Board of Works in the famine years' in *Historical Journal*, xiii, 4 (1970), p. 635.
[56] *Irish journals of Elizabeth Smith* p. 39.
[57] *Correspondence explanatory of the measures adopted*, Routh to Trevelyan, 16 Apr. 1846.
[58] Bowen, *Souperism*, pp 12 and 192.
[59] Bowen, *Protestant crusade*, p. 182.
[60] *Irish journals of Elizabeth Smith*, 21 Jan. 1847, p. 125.
[61] M. W. Flinn, 'Malthus, emigration and potatoes in the Scottish north-west, 1770-1870', in L. M. Cullen and T. C. Smout (ed.), *Comparative aspects of Scottish and Irish economic and social history*, (Edinburgh 1978), pp 47-64 and T. C. Smout, 'Famine and famine relief in Scotland', in Cullen and Smout op. cit. pp 21-31. For England in the 1840s see John Foster, *Class struggle and the industrial revolution. Early industrial capitalism in three English towns* (1977 ed.).
[62] Trevelyan, *Irish crisis*, p. 1.
[63] Norman Gash, *Mr. Secretary Peel*, (London 1961) p. 223.
[64] Norman Gash, *Sir Robert Peel*, (London 1976) p. 534.
[65] Ibid., p. 553.
[66] Kevin B. Nowlan, 'The political background', in Edwards and Williams, *Great famine*, p. 141.
[67] I do not intend to discuss the political events of the famine years in any detail. These are thoroughly dealt with in Kevin B. Nowlan's essay, referred to in the above footnote.

[68] O'Neill, 'Administration of relief', in Edwards and Williams, *Great famine*, p. 222, and Gash, *Sir Robert Peel*, p. 609.
[69] O'Neill, 'Administration of relief', p. 222.
[70] Quoted in Gash, *Sir Robert Peel*, p. 610.
[71] Harper, 'Entitlements', App. and Gash, *Sir Robert Peel*, p. 622.
[72] O'Neill, 'Administration of relief', p. 213.
[73] Ibid., p. 221.
[74] Ibid., pp 215-6.
[75] *Correspondence explanatory of the measures adopted*, Dobree to Trevelyan, 5 June 1846.
[76] Bourke, 'Irish grain trade', in *I.H.S.* 20 (1976) p. 163.
[77] O'Neill, 'Administration of relief', p. 227.
[78] *Correspondence explanatory of the measures adopted*, Pole to Trevelyan, 18 April 1846.
[79] O'Neill 'Administration of relief', pp 223-4.
[80] Trevelyan, *Irish crisis*, p. 30.
[81] *Relief of distress*, Trevelyan to Jones, 5 Oct. 1846.
[82] O'Neill, 'Administration of relief', p. 225 and *Relief of distress*, Trevelyan to Jones 22 Dec. 1846.
[83] Ibid., William Fraser, 10 Oct. 1846.
[84] Maurice R. O'Connell (ed.), *The correspondence of Daniel O'Connell*, viii, 1846-7, (Dublin 1980), letter no. 3301, 8 Oct. 1846, p. 111.
[85] *Relief of distress*, Russell to Redcliff, 15 Aug. 1846.
[86] Ibid., Rev. Theobald Mathew to Trevelyan, 20 Nov. 1846.
[87] *Society of Friends*, p. 57.
[88] Griffiths, 'The Irish Board of Works in the famine years', p. 635.
[89] *Relief of distress*, pp 78-9.
[90] *Correspondence explanatory of the measures adopted*, 21 Mar. 1846.
[91] Ibid., Board of Works to Trevelyan, 7 April 1846.
[92] *Relief of distress, July 1846 to January 1847.*
[93] *Correspondence explanatory of the measures adopted*, Jones to Earl of Lincoln, 9 April 1846.
[94] Ibid., 21 Mar. 1846.
[95] Ibid., 23 Mar. 1846.
[96] *Relief of distress*, Jones to Trevelyan 5 July 1846.
[97] Calculated from the table in *Relief of distress*, pp 78-9.
[98] *Correspondence explanatory of the measures adopted*, Jones to Earl of Lincoln, 9 April 1846.
[99] *Relief of distress*, 31 Aug. 1846.
[100] Ibid., Goodmill to Jones, 31 Aug. 1846.
[101] Griffiths 'The Irish Board of Works in the famine years', p. 637.
[102] Ibid., pp 641-2.
[103] *Relief of distress*, Jones to Trevelyan, 22 Sept. 1846.
[104] O'Neill, 'Administration of relief', in Edwards and Williams, *Great famine*, p. 231.
[105] *Relief of distress*, Trevelyan to Labouchere, 6 Oct. 1846.
[106] O'Neill, 'Administration of relief', p. 236.
[107] *Relief of distress*, 14 Dec. 1846.
[108] Ibid., Hyde to Mason, 9 Dec. 1846.
[109] Ibid., Denis McKenny, p. 220.
[110] *Relief of distress*, Jones to Routh, 21 Dec. 1846.
[111] Ibid., 20 Dec. 1846.

[112] Ibid., Jones to Trevelyan, 18 Oct. 1846.
[113] Ibid., Edmund Wynne, 8 Nov. 1846.
[114] Ibid., Wynne to Jones, 26 Nov. 1846.
[115] *Society of Friends*, p. 35.
[116] *Relief of distress*, 5 Dec. 1846.
[117] *Society of Friends*, p. 161.
[118] *Correspondence, Jan. to March, relief of distress*, Jones to Trevelyan, 13 Jan. 1847.
[119] *Relief of distress*, Jones to Trevelyan, 26 Nov. 1846.
[120] Griffiths, 'The Irish Board of Works in the famine years', pp 635 and 642.
[121] Harper, 'Entitlements', pp 31-2.
[122] *Relief of distress*, Sir Gaspard le Marchant, Tulla, Co. Clare, to the Military Secretary, 6 Nov. 1846.
[123] *Correspondence, Jan. to March, relief of distress*, Jones to Trevelyan, 19 Jan. 1847.
[124] Ibid., Wynne to Walker, 12 Jan. 1847.
[125] Ibid., Gisborne to Walker, 27 Jan. 1847.
[126] Griffiths, 'The Irish Board of Works in the famine years', p. 649.
[127] *Correspondence, Jan. to March, relief of distress*, Wynne to Walker, 5 Jan. 1847.
[128] *Relief of distress*, Jones to Trevelyan, 21 Dec. 1846; *Correspondence Jan. to March, relief of distress*, 19 Jan. 1847.
[129] Ibid., Mulvany to Trevelyan, 27 Feb. 1847.
[130] O'Neill, 'Administration of relief', p. 237.
[131] Ibid., pp 231-2.
[132] Hickey, 'Three peninsular parishes', p. 408.
[133] *Society of Friends*, p. 440, App. XXII.
[134] *Relief of distress*, p. 109.
[135] Ibid., 7 Sept. 1846.
[136] Nowlan, 'The political background', in Edwards and Williams, *Great famine*, p. 138.
[137] Donnelly, *Cork*, p. 87.
[138] *Relief of distress*, 8 Oct. 1846.
[139] Ibid., Sir Gaspard le Marchant, Tulla, Co. Clare, 5 Nov. 1846.
[140] Ibid., 10 Dec. 1846.
[141] Ibid., 24 Oct. 1846.
[142] Ancel B. Keys, *The biology of human starvation*, (Minneapolis, 1950), pp 789 and 793-4.
[143] O'Neill 'Administration of relief', in Edwards and Williams, *Great famine*, p. 234.
[144] Harper, 'Entitlements', Table 4.
[145] *Society of Friends*, p. 59.
[146] O'Neill, 'Administration of relief', pp 239-41.
[147] *Society of Friends*, p. 55.
[148] Ibid., pp 35 and 67.
[149] Ibid., p. 127.
[150] Joseph Robins, *The lost children. A study of charity children in Ireland, 1700-1900*, (Dublin, 1980), p. 170.
[151] Christine Kinealy, 'The Irish Poor Law, 1838-1862. A study of the relationship between the local and central administrations'. Unpublished Ph.D. thesis, Dublin University 1984. p. 92.
[152] *Annual report of the commissioners for administering the laws for relief of the poor in Ireland. First report*, 1847-8, 963, xxxiii.
[153] Robins, *Lost children*, p. 181.
[154] James H. Tuke, *A visit to Connaught in the autumn of 1847* (London 1848), p. 27.
[155] Robins, *Lost children*, p. 173.

156 *Poor law commissioners, report 1847,*para. 35.
157 Kinealy 'Poor Law' p. 214.
158 James H. Tuke, *A visit,* p. 15.
159 *Poor law commissioners, report,* 1849, para. 21.
160 Trevelyan, *Irish crisis* quoted in Kinealy, 'Poor Law' p. 236.
161 Tuke *A visit,* p. 4.
162 Kinealy, 'Poor Law' p. 179.
163 Tuke, *A visit,* p. 28.
164 Kinealy, 'Poor Law' p. 146.
165 James Donnelly, Jr. 'The journals of Sir John Benn-Walsh relating to the management of his Irish estates, 1823-64' in *Cork Hist. Soc. Jn.* lxxx, (1974), pp 106-7.
166 *Poor law commissioners, report* 1847, App. A.
167 Kinealy, 'Poor Law', p. 176.
168 Quoted in Kinealy, 'Poor Law' p. 234.
169 Ibid., p. 242.
170 Donnelly, 'The journals of Sir John Benn-Walsh', p. 107.
171 Joel Mokyr, 'The deadly fungus: An econometric investigation into the short-term demographic impact of the Irish famine, 1846-1851', in *Research in population economics* 2, (1980) pp 237-77. Boyle and O Grada, 'Fertility trends', p. 26.
172 Mokyr, 'Deadly fungus', p. 268.
173 S. H. Cousens, 'The regional variation in mortality during the great Irish famine', in *R.I.A. Proc.* 63, (Sect. C), no. 3, (Feb. 1963) p. 141.
174 S. H. Cousens, 'Regional death rates in Ireland during the great famine from 1846 to 1851' in *Population studies,* pp 55-74, and Cousens, 'Regional variation', pp 127-49.
175 Boyle and O Grada, 'Fertility trends', p. 26.
176 Sir William P. MacArthur, 'Medical history of the famine' in Edwards and Williams, *Great famine,* p. 289.
177 Sen. *Poverty and famine,* p. 206.
178 MacArthur, 'Medical history of the famine' p. 290.
179 Keys, *Biology of human starvation,* p. 758.
180 Sen, op. cit. p. 215.
181 MacArthur, 'Medical history', pp 289-90.
182 Ibid., p. 291.
183 Cousens, 'Regional variations', p. 132 and Hickey, 'Four peninsular parishes', p. 446.
184 MacArthur 'Medical history', pp 306-8.
185 Cousens, 'Regional variations', p. 127.
186 Ibid., pp 139-48.
187 Boyle and O Grada, 'Fertility trends', footnote 15, p. 34.
188 Cousens, 'Regional death rates', p. 65.
189 Hickey, 'Four peninsular parishes', p. 608.
190 Zara Stein, Mervyn Susser, Gerhardt Saenger, Francis Marolla, *Famine and human development,* pp 73-79 and 224-9.
191 MacArthur, 'Medical history', p. 289.
192 Hickey, 'Four peninsular parishes', p. 418.
193 Thomson and McGusty (ed.), *Irish journals,* p. 148.
194 Quoted by Wilde in 1851, *Population Ireland,* p. 309.
195 *Relief of distress,* 23 July 1846.
196 Keys, *Biology of human starvation,* pp 777 and 790.
197 MacArthur, 'Medical history', p. 303.
198 Robins, *Lost children,* pp 194-5.

[199] Mokyr, 'Deadly fungus', p. 246.
[200] Oliver McDonagh, 'Irish emigration to the United States of America and the British colonies during the famine', in Edwards and Williams, *Great famine*, pp 320-1 and 331.
[201] O Grada, 'Across the briny ocean', p. 127 and McDonagh, op. cit. p. 325.
[202] David Fitzpatrick, *Irish emigration, 1801-1921*, (Dublin, 1984), pp 18-20.
[203] Donnelly (ed.), *The journals of Sir John Benn-Walsh'*, pp 103-6.
[204] McDonagh, 'Irish emigration', p. 334.
[205] Fitzpatrick, *Irish emigration*, p. 18.
[206] Mokyr, 'Deadly fungus', p. 250.
[207] McDonagh, 'Irish emigration', p. 366.
[208] O Grada, 'Across the briny ocean', pp 123, 126.
[209] John Locke (of Rathmines), *Ireland. Observations on the people, the land and the law in 1851 with special reference to the policy, practices and results of the Incumbered Estates Court* (Dublin 1852) p. 3. Padraig Lane, 'The encumbered estates court in Ireland, 1848-59' in *Economic and social review*, iii, (1972), p. 432.
[210] *Irish journals of Elizabeth Smith*, p 97.
[211] F. S. L. Lyons, (ed.), 'Vicissitudes of a middleman in Co. Leitrim' in *I.H.S.* ix, (1955) pp 300-18.
[212] *Return from the courts of queen's bench, common pleas, and exchequer in Ireland, of the number of ejectments brought in those courts for the last three years, beginning with Hilary term 1846 and ending with Hilary term 1849 etc.* 1849, (315), xlix, 235. *Return by provinces and counties (compiled from returns made to the inspector general of the Royal Irish Constabulary), of cases of actions which have come to the knowledge of the constabulary in each of the years from 1849 to 1880 inclusive,* 1881, (185), lxxvii 725.
[213] *Returns from registrar's office of the court of chancery in Ireland, of the number of causes, description of property, rental of estates, arrears of rent, when receiver was appointed etc. . . . in each county in Ireland during the years 1844, 1845 and 1846 and up to the 1st day of December 1847 etc.* 1847-8 (226), lvii, 213.
[214] *Reports and returns relating to evictions in the Kilrush Union*, 1849 (1089), xlix.
[215] Donnelly, *Cork*, p. 114.
[216] Beames, *Peasants and power*, pp 213-6.
[217] Cousens, 'Regional variations in mortality', p. 134.
[218] *Reports and returns . . . Kilrush Union.*
[219] Lane, 'Encumbered estates court', p. 443.
[220] Lane, 'The management of estates by financial corporations in Ireland after the famine' in *Studia Hibernica*, xiv, (1974) pp 67-89.
[221] Cecil Woodham-Smith, *The great hunger, Ireland 1845-9* (London 1962), is a noted example of this type of analysis.
[222] Philip Magnus, *Gladstone* (London, 1954).

EPILOGUE (pp 117-118)

[1] J. M. Goldstrom, 'Irish agriculture and the great famine', in Goldstrom and Clarkson (ed.), *Ir. population*, pp 155-172 is a useful resume of the debate.
[2] Cormac O Grada, 'Irish agricultural output before and after the famine' in *Jn. European Econ. Hist.* (Spring, 1984), pp 151-4.
[3] T. Barrington, 'A review of Irish agricultural prices' in *Statistical and social inquiry society jnl.*, part ci, vol. xv (1926-7) p. 251.

[4] *Agricultural statistics of Ireland 1910,* (C. 5964).
[5] J. S. Donnelly, 'The agricultural depression of 1859-64' in *Irish Econ. & Soc. Hist.* iii, (1976).
[6] Donnelly, *Cork,* p. 220.
[7] B. M. Walsh, 'Marriage rates and population pressure, Ireland 1871 and 1911' in *Econ. Hist. Rev.,* xxiii, (1970) pp 153-4.
[8] Charles R. Browne, 'The ethnography of Ballycroy Co. Mayo', plus similar articles on Garumna, Carna, Lettermullen, Clare Island, in *R.I.A. Proc.,* 1893-1902.
[9] Cormac O Grada, 'Some aspects of nineteenth-century Irish emigration', in Cullen and Smout, (ed.), *Comparative aspects of Scottish and Irish economic and social history* refutes the earlier analysis of S. H. Cousens, 'Emigration and demographic change in Ireland, 1851-1861' in *Econ. Hist. Rev.,* xiv, (1961) pp 275-88 and 'The regional variations in population changes in Ireland, 1861-81', ibid., xvii, (1964) pp 301-21.
[10] *Agricultural statistics of Ireland 1910,* (C. 5964).
[11] Cousens, 'Regional variations in population change', p. 310.
[12] Ibid., p. 319.
[13] P. M. A. Bourke, 'Uncertainties in the statistics of farm size in Ireland, 1841-51, *Statistical and social inquiry society of Ireland, jnl.,* xx, (1959-60), pp 20-26.
[14] Lane, 'Encumbered estates court', p. 442.
[15] J. W. Boyle, 'A marginal figure: the Irish agricultural labourer', in Sam Clark and James S. Donnelly Jr. (ed.), *Irish peasants: violence and political unrest, 1780-1914.* (Manchester, 1983), pp 316-7.
[16] Donnelly, *Cork,* p. 228.
[17] *Sixth report of the medical office of the privy council.* App. 6. Report by Dr. Edward Smith on the food of the labouring classes in England, 1864 (3416), xxviii, pp 282-329.
[18] The key works on this topic are Paul Bew, *Land and the national question in Ireland, 1858-82.* (Dublin, 1978) and Sam Clark, *Social origins of the Irish land war,* (Princeton, 1979).
[19] David W. Miller, 'Irish catholicism and the great famine' in, *Journal of Social History,* ix, (1975), pp 81-98.
[20] Sean Connolly, *Priests and people in pre-famine Ireland* (Dublin, 1982).
[21] Eugen Weber, *Peasants into Frenchmen* (London, 1977) p. 472.
[22] Eugene Hynes, 'The great hunger and Irish catholicism' in *Societas,* (1978), pp 137-156.
[23] The phrase 'devotional revolution' was coined by Emmet Larkin in his article, 'The devotional revolution in Ireland, 1850-75' in *A.H.R.* lxxvii, (1972), pp 625-652. For some evidence of pre-famine reform see James O'Shea, *Priests, politics and society in post-famine Ireland. A study of Co. Tipperary, 1850-91.* (Dublin, 1983), pp 30-36.
[24] Cecil Woodham-Smith, *The great hunger,* pp 412-413.
[25] Robert Kee, *Ireland. A history* (London *1980*).
[26] Quoted in Roger McHugh, 'The famine in oral tradition', in Edwards and Williams, *Great famine,* pp 434-5.
[27] Mary Carbery (ed.), *The farm by Lough Gur,* pp 58-66.

NOTE ON FURTHER READING

The two standard works on the famine are R. Dudley Edwards and T. Desmond Williams (ed.), *The great famine* (Dublin 1956) and Cecil Woodham-Smith, *The great hunger, Ireland 1845-9* (London 1962). The chapters dealing with pre-famine economic background in the former book are now seriously out of date, but it still contains valuable sections, notably on the political background, medical history and folklore. Cecil Woodham-Smith's book paints a highly dramatic and emotive picture of the famine. It is valuable for its graphic description of events but is unduly inclined to hold one person, Trevelyan, responsible for the shortcomings of government policy. Joel Mokyr's book, *Why Ireland starved* (London 1983), despite its title is not a history of the famine, rather a highly ambitious analysis of pre-famine economy and society. Much of it is controversial, but the book should be read by all serious students of this period. The book also contains a very comprehensive bibliography. For a resumé of the current state of Irish population history see Joel Mokyr and Cormac O Grada, 'New developments in Irish population history, 1700-1850', in *Econ. Hist. Rev.*, xxvii, no. 4, (Nov. 1984). Readers in search of further material should consult the footnotes of this book.